EDUCATIONAL THOUGHT
An Introduction

MODERN REVIVALS IN PHILOSOPHY

Series Editor: Dr David Lamb

David Archard
Marxism and Existentialism: The
Political Philosophy of Sartre and
Merleau-Ponty
(0 7512 0051 4)

Jorge A Larrain
Marxism and Ideology
(0 7512 0013 1)

Jorge A Larrain
A Reconstruction of Historical
Materialism
(0 7512 0048 4)

Jorge A Larrain
The Concept of Ideology
(0 7512 0049 2)

D G C Macnabb
David Hume: His Theory of Knowledge
and Morality
(0 7512 0014 X)

Anthony O'Hear
Experience, Explanation and Faith
(0 7512 0052 2)

Stephen Priest (ed)
Hegel's Critique of Kant
(0 7512 0064 6)

George J Stack
Kierkegaard's Existential Ethics
(0 7512 0018 2)

George J Stack
Sartre's Philosophy of Social Existence
(0 7512 0058 1)

W H Walsh
Metaphysics
(0 7512 0019 0)

W H Walsh
Reason and Experience
(0 7512 0020 4)

John Wilson
Logic and Sexual Morality
(0 7512 0101 4)

Antony Flew
Essays on Logic and Language
(0 7512 0115 4) 2 volume set

G J Warnock
Berkeley
(0 7512 0118 9)

Desmond Paul Henry
That Most Subtle Question (Quaestio
Subtilissima)
(0 7512 0128 6)

Desmond Paul Henry
The Logic of Saint Anselm
(0 7512 0130 8)

R F Atkinson
Sexual Morality
(0 7512 0158 8)

G H R Parkinson
Spinoza's Theory of Knowledge
(0 7512 0159 6)

William Lyons
Emotion
(0 7512 0132 4)

Roy Edgley
Reason in Theory and Practice
(0 7512 0179 0)

Frank Jackson
Perception: A Representative Theory
(0 7512 0190 1)

Joseph McCarney
The Real World of Ideology
(0 7512 0191 X)

David McLellan
The Young Hegelians and Karl Marx
(0 7512 0178 2)

Anthony Skillen
Ruling Illusions: Philosophy and The
Social Order
(0 7512 0200 2)

J N Findlay
Hegel: A Re-examination
(0 7512 0180 4)

Bernard Bosanquet
The Philosophical Theory of the State
(0 7512 0204 5)

Joseph Needham
Moulds of Understanding: A Pattern of
Natural Philosophy
(0 7512 0209 6)

Frank E Manuel
Shapes of Philosophical History
(0 7512 0210 X)

Benjamin Gibbs
Freedom and Liberation
(0 7512 0214 2)

Richard Norman and Sean Sayers
Hegel, Marx and Dialectic: A Debate
(0 7512 0219 3)

Robin Attfield
God and the Secular: The Philosophical
Assessment of Secular Reasoning from
Bacon to Kant
(0 7512 0243 6)

EDUCATIONAL THOUGHT
An Introduction

Brenda Almond

Professor of Moral and Social Philosophy
University of Hull

First published in Great Britain in 1969 by
Macmillan and Company Ltd

Reprinted in 1993 by
Gregg Revivals
Gower House
Croft Road
Aldershot
Hampshire GU11 3HR
England

Gregg Revivals
Distributed in the United States by
Ashgate Publishing Company
Old Post Road
Brookfield
Vermont 05036
USA

British Library Cataloguing in Publication Data

Almond, Brenda
  Educational Thought: Introduction. - New
  ed. - (Modern Revivals in Philosophy
  Series)
  I. Title II. Series
  370.1

  ISBN 0-7512-0264-9

Printed in Great Britain by The Ipswich Book Co. Ltd

TO ANNA, LOUISE, PAULA AND MARTIN

Contents

Acknowledgements

I should like to thank the editors of this series, Professor and Mrs O'Connor, for their helpful comment and criticism.

1 Introduction

The charge is sometimes levelled against education that, as a body of knowledge or theory, it is vacuous; other fields, particularly the sciences, are concerned with hard material data, and where they have results, these are tangible and can readily be accepted by non-expert bystanders. But education is not so clear cut; its subject-matter is hard to define, and even where its theories produce results, it is a matter of controversy whether these results are to be described as success or failure.

So any discussion of educational theory must begin with a quest for the content of education, the subject-matter of educational theory; and only as a result of this search will it appear whether the charge of vacuity is well-levelled or not.

An obvious starting-point for such a search is the teacher, and most practising teachers can be persuaded by an interested inquirer to explain and justify their classroom techniques and policy – or, in the case of head teachers, the system they adopt in running their school. There is a sense, of course, in which what is provided by the answers they give to specific questions (on discipline and punishment, encouragement of learning, streaming and unstreaming, etc.) is the theoretical basis of their educational practice. However, although almost all teachers are educational theorists in this sense, two very different approaches are possible. On the one hand, there are those who justify their techniques on the basis of their own personal experience and the knowledge that they have acquired in the course of their career. On the other hand, there are those who are prepared to offer a justification in more general terms, and substantiate their views from a wider field than their own direct experience can afford.

The first kind of theory reduces to rules-of-thumb, which can only be accepted with reservations by others and used as guide-lines, since the personality of the individual teacher has been an important constant factor in their formulation. It is true that most practices, from plumbing or bricklaying to medicine and management, have rules-of-thumb, and these can be, and in the first two cases are sometimes, incorporated into helpful hand-books directed to others who might want to follow the same occupations. But the plumber and the bricklayer deal with material commodities, so that a tip that one bricklayer has found useful is likely to be of equal value to another. He has no need, therefore, to carry his investigations to any greater depth, or to try to discover why, in scientific terms, the practices he has found successful actually work. But the practitioner in the other fields mentioned, management and medicine, is, like the teacher, working with human material. This immediately increases the complexity of the situation, in so far as the reactions of human beings to the same treatment are not nearly so consistent as the re-actions of metal or mortar. Equally important, however, is the fact that in their dealings with human beings, the doctor, the manager or the teacher are themselves part of the situation they are trying to judge, and bring to it their own distinctive per-sonality. This means that the results that are obtained by one man using a particular method, and which he attributes to his use of that method, may in fact result from his own personality rather than from the method itself. Hence, while his advice may be of value to someone who resembles himself in whatever is the significant respect (and this itself is something it would be very difficult to determine), it might be positively detrimental to someone else who lacked that particular quality. So the recom-mendation of a particular manager, for instance, that anything less than a tough line will inevitably fail with the men in his particular industry, can safely be ignored by a different sort of person, whose democratic approach will not necessarily lead to the chaos and strikes the first manager predicts. In fact the view of the first manager is valuable, not because it reveals anything about the behaviour of men in his industry – it does not – but because it reveals something about the character of the man who makes the observation. Similarly, the theories of a teacher, based solely on his own experience, may reveal more about the teacher than about the general value of his methods. It is possible that some of the historical 'theories of education' amount to no more than these highly personal recommendations, but this is a question to return to later.

Instead, I want to consider the position of the second kind of teacher – the one who advances more general reasons for his own educational practice. What kind of reasons are these likely to be, and in what sense, if any, do they constitute a theory? In order to answer these questions, it is necessary to look critically at the word 'theory' itself, and to arrive at some kind of analysis of the term; this task is undertaken in the next chapter. In subsequent chapters, four of the most historically famous and influential theories of education are examined in order to establish their validity and the extent to which they meet the requirements of today's much stricter conception of a theory. In a final chapter, the relation of these historical theories to current trends and debates in education is discussed, and some continuing problems within education are considered in the light of the views of these earlier thinkers.

2 What is an Educational Theory?

Educationists do not – or should not – wish to live in academic isolation. If this is not to happen, then, despite the fact that educationists are frequently more concerned with policy-making than are other kinds of theorists, their use of the term 'theory' must be seen to have something in common with the term as used by, for example, scientists, mathematicians or philosophers. But it is not immediately obvious that these groups all use the word in exactly the same way. In fact, one broad division immediately presents itself: that between the scientific use of the term, and its use in literary or artistic appraisal. Some would demand separate mention of its use in the social sciences, but I think it will become clear from what follows that this is not a separate use, apart from the great complexity and variability of human material which has already been mentioned.

It will be useful, then, to compare the way the term is used in these two fields, looking first at the scientific use. Usually, when one speaks of a theory or explanation in the physical sciences, one is speaking of one of two things:

either 1. a unifying hypothesis, i.e. a general description of how things happen, from which all the particular incidents of which we are aware can be seen to follow. (The first type of theory starts from the particular incidents which are all that are known, and the scientist, by a process which involves a mental leap (a gap in the chain of strict reasoning from prosaic single facts to truths of universal application), suggests a general hypothesis which would account for them all. Newton's well-known discovery of the law of gravity was of this type: the many particular incidents of falling objects became part of an expected pattern on his gravitational hypothesis;)

or 2. a variation on this, by which particular incidents that appear to be exceptions to the general law are accommodated under another general law.

A good example of the second type of theory is an experiment described by J. M. Tanner in *Education and Physical Growth*[1].* The general law which was assumed in embarking upon the investigation (conducted by Widdowson in 1951) was that extra food for children at a time of scarcity would result in an increase in physical growth (height and weight). To find out the exact extent of this gain, two orphanages were used, orphanage *B* being given a food supplement after a six-month control period, while orphanage *A* continued throughout on normal rations. Tanner describes what happened: 'Though the *B* children actually gained more weight than the *A* children during the first unsupplemented six months, they gained less during the second six months, despite actually taking in a measured 20 per cent more calories.'

The explanation for this unexpected exception to the assumed general rule turned out to be that at precisely the six-month point a sister-in-charge transferred from *A* to become head of *B*, where she set up a system of iron rule, with meal-times particularly chosen as times for public rebuke.

The exception to the first assumed general law led, in this case, to a new general law accounting for the exception: that adverse psychological or emotional conditions outweigh actual food intake in affecting physical growth.

There are some aspects of current theory that follow this model – as, for instance, when the fact that children do better work when their efforts are praised rather than ignored is built into a general hypothesis about motivation. But this, strictly speaking, is a psychological theory rather than a purely educational one. In the same way, a general hypothesis about, for instance, the effects of different home backgrounds on children's school work is a sociological theory rather than an educational one. Neither are what, historically, has been meant by an educational theory, even though elements of psychological or

* Small numbers refer to notes at the end of the chapter.

sociological theory can be found in the works of the educational theorists of the past.

This is not to deny, of course, what is clearly the case: that relevant studies in psychology and sociology are essential and extremely significant for anyone interested in education, and for anyone responsible for determining any aspect of educational policy and practice, whether he is directly concerned as a teacher or administratively concerned in local or central government. At this stage, however, I shall avoid the temptation to include these studies within the concept of educational theory, and having isolated the notion to this extent, ask: Do the theories of the historical educational theorists fit any more readily the pattern of theories in art and literature?

In looking for a definition of theories of this type (i.e. literary or artistic), it is necessary first of all to set on one side those theories apparently within the fields of literature or art which are really empirical hypotheses similar to those with which the scientist works – as, for instance, a theory about the authorship of Shakespeare's plays, or of certain books in the Bible, or of the method employed by a Renaissance painter in producing his works of art. These fall into a different category of theories which follow the same pattern of hypothesis supported by particular pieces of evidence as in some scientific theories.

The theories which at first glance appear to differ entirely in form from scientific ones are those which are to be found in books about, for instance, the Novel or Drama. In the case of the former one would find perhaps that certain elements of the Novel, such as Form and Content, Plot and Character, are isolated and discussed in highly general terms, so that the conclusion reached by the writer will apply equally to any novel, and not merely to the one or more he may cite in his discussion.

Statements with even less particular application than this may also be made by writers on literature: as an example, one could cite this statement by R. Liddell, made in the course of a discussion on the place of summary in the Novel, 'Fiction is a rhetorical art, and seeks to communicate feelings quite as much as Sense – and Feeling is not to be communicated in a bare summary'.[2]

In addition to these theories within literary criticism or aesthetics, there are theories on a still higher level of generality concerning the nature of literature or art; as, for instance, the view that they are modes of self-expression; or, in contrast to this, the Marxist theory that art and literature issue from the economic situation and reflect the class struggle.

One can now begin to see what is the function of theories in these fields. Essentially, I would suggest, it is this: that where there exists a mass of particular data – particular novels, pictures, plays, poems – the theories attempt to abstract some general principles from these unlimited particularities. What they offer, in fact, is a way of unifying the data, structuring it and discovering a pattern within it. Again, since the data are limitless and beyond the scope of any human being, the pattern has to be inferred from the limited data available to any particular theorist (the books he has read, the paintings or sculpture he has seen) rather than deduced from the totality, all literature or all art. Nevertheless, the pattern he has discerned or posited will be held to apply to the whole.

If this conclusion regarding the nature of theories in art and literature is compared with the definition of scientific theories as unifying hypotheses, it will be seen that the appearance of total dissimilarity between them was deceptive. Even if it is agreed, though, that theories in both science and the arts are alike in the respect that both are definable as unifying hypotheses, it might appear that there are at least two respects in which they are too dissimilar for useful comparison.

One is that scientific theories are used for purposes of prediction in a way in which literary theories are not. However, this is simply a consequence of scientific theories having a reference to events which, of course, occur in time and space, whereas literary theories have no such reference. Historical theories, on the other hand, do have this reference and, consequently, can be used for prediction; as, for instance, the Marxist interpretation of history is used to predict revolution.

A second and more serious difference is this: in the literary or artistic sphere the hypothesis is essentially *subjective*; what is offered is a way of looking at things which may be accepted or rejected according to its appeal to the person studying the theory. Scientific hypotheses, on the other hand, are discoveries, and the laws which the theoretical scientist discovers have *objective* validity. They have to be regarded as either true or false; personal preference is not involved.

It is at this point that it may be worth looking again at the picture of theory in science which was presented earlier. At one level, of course, it was perfectly correct; scientific theories are indeed confirmed or rejected on the basis of objective facts. However, it is also true that, whether confirmed or rejected, scientific theories are essentially *hypotheses*. In *The Logic of Scientific Discovery* (37)* Karl Popper used an argument which is not unacceptable to scientists and which places the hypotheses of science on a pragmatic plane. Popper recognised that as long as the hypotheses of science were regarded as general laws which were true or false, and could be proved or disproved, there were serious difficulties, of a philosophical nature, as to how we could be said to know any of these general laws of science. For there seemed to be only two acceptable ways of knowing things, neither of which applied to the general laws of science. First, one could know logical truths by a process of deductive proof, since these follow purely from the rules one is using; for example, one could know that *if* all metals expand when heated, and *if* gold is a metal, *then* gold will expand when heated. And, secondly, one could in some sense know immediate truths of experience, such as that one is looking at a brown table-top or hearing a loud noise. The general laws of science, however, are neither immediate truths of experience (and, taken as having universal application they are beyond anyone's experience, whether immediate or not) nor mere pieces of deduction, for they would only follow deductively from principles as broad and unverifiable as themselves. Popper's suggestion, then, is that we regard the general laws of science purely as hypotheses, and that we make no claims about their objective truth. On the other hand, we may well prove their objective falsity. For while no finite number of experiments will provide ultimate confirmation of a positive hypothesis, any hypothesis can at any

* Numbers in parenthesis refer to Bibliography, pages 105 ff.

stage be disproved by a single contrary instance.[3] A scientific hypothesis, then, provides a helpful and subjectively satisfying way of structuring the data of experience.

This view provides a better account of the history of science than the less sophisticated view from which we started. As long as the hypothesis that the sun moved round the earth accounted for all the facts that people were interested in, it was a more useful assumption than mere haphazard acceptance of the relative motions of sun and stars. But the Copernican hypothesis of the central position of the sun, which displaced this, accounted for the great complexity of facts of which astronomers were then becoming aware. A similar revolution in accepted ways of thinking took place with Einstein, and once again a radically new hypothesis displaced the old.

If this account of scientific theory is accepted, then it is not difficult to reconcile with the account of other types of theory that have been offered. In all cases, the significant contribution of theory is to provide a policy for practice (in the case of science to suggest a line for experiment) by imposing a pattern on the unruly mass of data and facts which present themselves in any field, and supplying a unifying way of looking at those data. But again in all fields, the value of the pattern is pragmatic; as the line suggested is followed, the scheme may prove inadequate to meet the new facts that are uncovered, and the function of original thinkers in any field is to suggest new and more adequate ways of structuring the total available data.

Applying these findings to education, one can see what is, or should be, the task of the educational theorist. The data with which the educationist is concerned are, in ascending order of generality, *the curriculum* (the particular content of the school day), *the organisation of the school* itself, and *society's arrangements for education* as a whole, and in all its aspects. But just as the writer on the Novel might turn from talk about particular examples; and just as the scientist may in theorising leave aside specific results in order to talk about a subject in concept, as an abstraction (talking, for instance, about 'gravity' or 'nuclear fission' instead of the particular result of his experiments in these fields) so the educationist may in theorising write about

B

and discuss the curriculum or the school or the education system as an abstraction, offering a model for imitation rather than a commentary on what exists. Examples of both types of activity are to be found in writings on education.

For example, L. G. W. Sealey and V. Gibbon, in *Communication and Learning in the Primary School*, are clearly offering, in precisely the fashion suggested, a unifying way of looking at the primary school curriculum, so often seen as a mere conglomeration of 'subjects', arbitrarily put together on a time-table, when they say:

One way of looking at children's activities in primary schools is to consider it in terms of a system of communication that is multi-directional. That which is communicated is experience. . . .[4]

Sealey and Gibbon are suggesting here a novel and useful approach to primary education in which normal subject-boundaries are transcended, and every activity is looked upon as a form of communication between the child and the outside world – in other words, they are presenting an educational theory.

This element of recommendation which appears in educational theories can be described as THE VALUE-ELEMENT, since it implies that something worthwhile can replace what exists already, by practical efforts on the part of those who desire it. The description of the worthwhile objective could be described as THE IDEAL ELEMENT, and, in the case of different theorists, this may have metaphysical, religious, political or ideological facets.

The actual data themselves, the facts of educational life, which provide the starting-point for any educational theory, provide a third element, THE EMPIRICAL. As far as this empirical element is concerned, it is essential to remember that it is insufficient by itself; to have a theory, as opposed to a collection of facts, it is necessary to move from the empirical to the conceptual level, even if only to return there in the end. That is to say, for example, that the sociologist who has gathered facts about the effects of eleven plus selection on particular children, only presents a theory when, on the basis of those facts, he makes statements of a general nature, such as, for instance, that selection reinforces social class differences.

There is an influential school of thought, which lays stress on the empirical element of educational theory, to the extent even of suggesting that it is its only valid component. A strong case for this point of view was made by D. J. O'Connor in *An Introduction to the Philosophy of Education* (35). O'Connor approached the question from an empirical viewpoint not very different from the one that has been offered here, first of all considering the role of explanation in science, and then applying his findings to the question of the social sciences in general and to education in particular. His account of a scientific theory as a confirmed hypothesis or set of confirmed hypotheses fulfilling the three functions of description, prediction and explanation is also in agreement with the view put forward here, but differs in the stress that is placed on the objective nature of scientific theories.

Fundamentally, O'Connor's position is this: that teachers today need a basis of sound scientific theory from which to work. He suggests that, whereas in the past the relatively simple truths which teachers could reach on the basis of their own observations were perhaps adequate for the relatively uncomplicated situations in which they found themselves, the complexity of modern life in urban and industrial societies makes their position now to some extent analogous to that of doctors or engineers. All three are pre-scientific professions, so that in the past practitioners in all three fields have operated without the background of scientific knowledge which is taken for granted today. However, the kind of achievements of which doctors and engineers are capable now would not have been possible on the basis of the 'trial-and-error' method of building up knowledge which was the mark of the pre-scientific centuries. On the contrary, it is the activities of research scientists, for instance in discovering antibiotics, which have brought success to activities which previously could only have met with failure. Similarly, O'Connor suggests, teaching based on any pre-scientific psychology (and here he mentions the views of Pestalozzi, Froebel and Montessori) is based on something little better than guesswork. In its place, teachers need principles based on sound psychological and sociological principles which can be supported by experimental findings. O'Connor recognises the qualifications with which such a view must be held; in particular he points to the limitations of psychology and sociology as sciences resulting from the complexity of their object of study, human or animal behaviour, and human society. Nevertheless, he insists that the only valid type of educational theory consists of recommendations for educational practice based on experimental findings in the social sciences.

This type of application is, of course, an important aspect of education, but there are two important respects in which it is unsatisfactory as an account of what educational theory is or should be. In the first place, it would appear to impose unnecessary and even undesirable limitations on the activities of educational thinkers. It restricts possible innovations in the educational field to improvements in techniques within the existing system. On this view, for instance, it would be legitimate educational theorising to suggest ways of improving eleven plus selection, but not to argue in favour of a comprehensive system except on grounds of efficiency. To conceive of a radically new type of school, after the fashion of A. S. Neill, would not count as educational theory.

On the other hand, while O'Connor's theory imposes these limitations on educational theory, it might at the same time be held to stretch unreasonably the functions of psychology and sociology within education. In an article called 'Preface to an Autonomous Discipline of Education' (53), F. MacMurray argues that, far from becoming parts of educational theory, psychology and sociology in their educational aspects remain essentially parts of their own discipline. Merely by being set in the classroom their inquiries, he suggests do not become 'educational', and they do not tell us how to teach or what to teach. 'We cannot,' he says, 'expect a true discipline of education to arise simply by localizing the questions of some other discipline within a school setting.'

MacMurray is not arguing in favour of a form of educational theory based on any speculative system of philosophy (idealism, realism, pragmatism, etc.) but rather on one based on a critical and analytic philosophy like O'Connor's. Nevertheless, he thinks that such a philosophy can permit a broader conception of educational theory. The meaning he wants to attach to the term can be seen in his definition of an educational problem: '. . . . a problem in theory of education is a search for reasoned ideas about what kind of deliberate culturation will react with existent beliefs and predispositions to modify a learner's personality and thereby increase his effectiveness in dealings with himself and his world.' (By the term 'culturation' MacMurray means learning of the skills, ideas, information and attitudes of a culture.)

Both MacMurray's and O'Connor's views have been criticised in an article by P. Hirst called 'Philosophy and Educational Theory' (52). Because of the importance of these criticisms it is worth considering this article in some detail. The three views of the relation between philosophy and education which have already been referred to here are classified by Hirst as:

1. The traditional view that certain philosophies entail certain educational systems.
2. The view that there is an autonomous discipline of education which draws on philosophical beliefs while not being determined by them.
3. The view, particularly put forward by O'Connor, that philosophy has a purely critical and clarificatory function in education.

The first view is criticised by Hirst on several grounds: first, because it overlooks the essential factual considerations (psychological and sociological) which must play a part in determining educational practice, a point which has been accepted and stressed in the discussion so far. Secondly, because it suggests a formal deductive relation, where in fact the conclusions of educational practice are too vague and too multitudinous to be based on any limited sets of premises. Hirst says, 'It is rather that in the midst of a complex network of understanding which cannot be adequately and formally expressed, we form our judgements, and in the statements which we use to express our reasons, draw attention to the major considerations which have influenced us.' Finally, Hirst points out that educational views and philosophical beliefs often seem to be independent of each other, in that people with the same beliefs may have different educational principles (e.g. the differing views of Christians on religious education in schools) and also people with opposing beliefs of a philosophical nature nevertheless may share identical educational views. These are all valid criticisms which can usefully be borne in mind when studying any of the educational philosophers of the past.

However, it is less easy to agree with Hirst when he goes on to criticise the other two theories concerning the relation between philosophy and education. Far from accepting that a common claim to the term 'theory' implies (as has been argued here) some common principle or procedure, Hirst considers that it is, in fact, a defining feature of an autonomous discipline that it has its own distinctive and unique type of judgement; that is to say, on Hirst's view, what makes a scientific theory a theory is quite different from what makes an historical theory a theory. He describes both kinds of explanation as *sui generis* and unique in character, and he suggests that, in the same way, this may be true of moral judgements. This is not the place to discuss this view of historical explanation, particularly as Hirst does not consider educational theory to be an autonomous discipline even in this sense. But it may be noted that his view of autonomous disciplines makes all standards internal to the discipline in question, and entails that comparisons of truth or falsity across the disciplines cannot be made – scientific truth is of one sort, and historical truth another. It will be seen that on this criterion there is very little that could not claim to be autonomous discipline, including even such 'sciences' as astrology or phrenology.

Hirst has made this point only in order to suggest that there is yet another different type of theory which follows a pattern closer to that of educational theory. This is the type of theory that is contained in the judgements of political or social theory, judgements which are 'practical judgements as to what ought to be done . . . made on the basis of much knowledge and experience', and drawing on a variety of specialist disciplines.

He states this view more fully as follows:

I would suggest that educational theory is one of a group of related theories each concerned with making similar forms of judgement, much in the same way as the physical sciences form a related group. It is their concern to answer questions about intentional practical activities by making practical judgements that distinguishes this group of theories from other groups. And within this group it is the particular constellation of activities we label 'educational' that determines in the first place the scope of educational theory.

Hirst goes on to add that it is the type of questions it seeks to answer which marks out the field of educational theory.

The reader may have observed that this view is not very different from that of the 'practising teacher' hypothesised earlier, in avoiding the question of what is to be held as a valid conclusion, or who is to make the observations which will be made the basis of practice. In other words, by deliberately cutting off education from anything resembling scientific standards of truth or validity, Hirst is, in fact, returning the subject to its traditional status as a field where all may propound their ideas with as complete a freedom and as much imagination as in the past.

Having offered this view of educational theory, Hirst goes on to discuss the third category he has mentioned, O'Connor's view that the function of philosophy within education is limited to criticism and analysis. Hirst accepts that these are the limits of philosophy, but suggests that educational thought can go further. He points out that educational discussion is usually not just empirical but includes value-judgements and appeal to metaphysical beliefs, and he is reluctant to admit that these actually detract from the value of the theories. He quotes O'Connor's statement that the word 'theory' as it is used in educational contexts is generally a courtesy title. It is justified only where we are applying well-established experimental findings in psychology or sociology to the practice of education,[5] and he comments: 'Because of his obsession with scientific theory as a paradigm for all theories, he totally mis-judges the importance of the non-scientific elements that he himself diagnoses in educational discussion . . . Educational theory is in the first place to be understood as the essential background to rational educational practice, not as a limited would-be scientific pursuit.' One further quotation makes it absolutely clear what is at issue between Hirst and O'Connor: 'The theories of science and the theories of practical activities are radically different in character because they perform quite different functions, they are constructed to do different jobs.'

This cleavage between scientific theories and the theories which determine practical decisions in education or politics or private life, is very far from the outlook of the empirically-minded man in any field, for whom the term 'unscientific' implies a root criticism of the standards and criteria that are being applied, even in such areas as education or politics.

But Hirst goes on to draw some conclusions regarding the function of philosophy in education from this. He says that he sees philosophy as a second-order activity, though one that is by no means insignificant in education. He regards it as tying together knowledge from various sources: if the issue is moral education, for example, then the relevant knowledge would derive from moral insight, religious beliefs, and from accounts of psychological development. He also sees philosophy as contributing certain matters of substance as, for instance, the analysis of moral judgements. Finally, Hirst recommends that philosophers of education should start from a consideration of educational practice and direct their attention to philosophical questions that arise from specific educational issues.

As far as this final recommendation goes, both Hirst and O'Connor would be in agreement; it is, in fact, the only view that it is possible to take of the function of a critical and analytic philosophy within education. It does, however, beg a question. Educational philosophy and educational theory are not necessarily interchangeable terms, and it does not follow from this view of the limited activities of the philosopher within education that educational theory must be an unscientific, unprovable, quasipolitical programme.

But neither does it follow that it must be limited to such things as a stark and pedestrian application of learning theory to the classroom situation. For it is, undeniably, a fact that education is neither static nor directionless, whether, metaphorically-speaking, anyone takes the driving-seat or not. Of possible candidates for the driver's role, the psychologist will deliberately abstain from any broad consideration of principle in his role as psychologist, and so too will the sociologist; his aim will be a dispassionate and descriptive assessment of the education system in its social aspects, an assessment which is neutral and free from value-judgements.[6] The teacher, again, is someone who finds himself working within a particular system, which he must take for granted in its broader perspective, even if it happens that he is one of the few courageous individuals who tackle a small aspect of the system (e.g. corporal punishment) on his own account, and without waiting for a general shift of opinion.

Historically, it was the ideas of certain thinkers and teachers that determined the direction of education and gave consideration to it in its wider aspects. These ideas are the educational theory of the past. One of the tasks of this book will be to consider the extent to which these theories fit into the framework outlined above, and how far they fall outside it.

SUMMARY

The view that educational theory consists simply of rules-of-thumb is discussed, and it is pointed out that these would, in a field such as education, be highly personal in application. Instead, educational theory is compared with other types of theory, such as those in science, art and literature. All of these types of theory can be seen as ways of unifying or structuring a wide variety of data. They are essentially hypotheses, which can never be conclusively verified even though they may be falsified. As hypotheses, they tend to point to a line of procedure for the future.

In an educational theory three elements can be isolated: a value element, an 'ideal' element and an empirical or factual element. The view that the empirical element is the only valid part of educational theory is rejected, as is the view that educational judgements are autonomous, unique in character and not subject to the same kind of standards of truth as scientific theories. It is concluded that educational theory must combine scientific accuracy with regard to its data, with conscious commitment to values and aims.

NOTES

1. Tanner (47), page 107.
2. Liddell (24), page 64.
3. To take a logician's illustration of this point: no matter how many swans were observed to be white, one could never finally prove the proposition that 'all swans are white'. But it would take only the discovery of a single black swan to show that this proposition was false.
4. Sealey & Gibbon (44), page 17.
5. O'Connor (35), page 110.
6. See Musgrave (32), page 123.

FURTHER READING

For further discussions on the nature of educational theory, see the articles by Hirst (52) and MacMurray (53). See also O'Connor (35), in particular chapter 5.

For Popper's views on the nature of scientific theory, see Popper (37).

3 Plato

For a unified view of Plato's theories about education, it is necessary to see these theories for what they were: a working out in concrete day-to-day detail of a total philosophy. In relation to Plato, the term 'philosophy' can be taken to mean a particular view as to the meaning and purpose of life, which determines both the answer to the individual's questions about what he should do, and also the questions of the politically-conscious about the way the state should be organised and governed.

At the risk of over-simplification, but in the interest of clarity, I would suggest a way of placing Plato's educational thought in the context of his general philosophical views.

'VIRTUE IS KNOWLEDGE'

The kernel of Plato's philosophy was his view that 'virtue is knowledge'. From this basic view stems on the one hand Plato's views about the nature of knowledge and about what it is that can be known, and on the other hand his views about moral conduct. On the first question, he concludes that knowledge is not a matter of appreciating or understanding what goes on in the sensible world, merely receiving the data of the five senses, but rather a matter of becoming aware of conceptual truths. This means understanding the relations between abstract principles, and the meaning of general ideas, such as, in the moral sphere, justice and truth; in the aesthetic sphere, beauty and symmetry; or, in the mathematical sphere, equality or triangularity. It is this theory which is well known under the alternative names of the THEORY OF FORMS or the THEORY OF IDEAS.

But the view that 'virtue is knowledge' is equally the basis of Plato's ethical theory, since it leads Plato to hold that all the separate moral virtues – courage, self-control, justice, etc. – are essentially not divisible from each other but are all aspects of a single concept, virtue. This unitary virtue is indeed knowledge, but it is knowledge of a very particular kind; it is knowledge of good and bad. Essentially, in fact, it is knowledge of *the* Good, in that it involves knowledge of the *Idea of the Good*.

Since virtue is essential for happiness (a proof of this is offered in the *Protagoras*) and since it is only possible for most people in the context of a particular social setting, these threads are brought together in the *Republic* in a description of the ideal political organisation, one aspect of which is the education of those who will run it.

SOCRATES

Before amplifying these ideas further, something must be said about the context in which Plato was writing. Socrates, whom Plato makes the leading figure in most of his dialogues, was one of the major influences on Plato's thought, and an understanding of Plato begins with an understanding of him.

Socrates was born in 470 BC in Athens, a Greek city-state economically based on a minimum of foreign slavery, but above that level exemplifying the best kind of democratic organisation. Socrates was familiar with earlier philosophies, but he did not wholly accept any of them. He was very much influenced by Orphic beliefs, particularly the notion that the body is a tomb, in which the soul is trapped for a time. According to the Orphic doctrine, the soul is released from one body by death only to be reborn in another – an inferior one in the case of a bad man, such as the body of an animal – a superior one in the case of a good man. But the ultimate aim of a series of good lives would be to gain release from what was called the 'wheel of birth and death'. The most general aspect of this type of philosophy is the notion that life is an evil, the body an encumbrance, and death something desirable. The opposite notion, that life is a good thing and something to be enjoyed till it is brought to an end by the evil, death, is also well represented in Greek philosophy but both Socrates and Plato preferred the ascetic view. Socrates did not accept the Orphic doctrines in all their detail, but in the *Apology* he expresses a qualified belief in the immortality of the soul, and elsewhere (in the *Phaedo*) describes the life of the philosopher as the practice of death, since it is only in death that the philosopher will be able to pursue his inquiries unhampered by any physical considerations. Plato, if not Socrates, definitely believed in Rebirth and also in the doctrine of Reminiscence, i.e. the belief that the soul could remember things from its pre-existence.

The most significant event in Socrates' life, indeed its turning-point, was a declaration of the Delphic oracle: that there was no one wiser than Socrates. According to his own report, from that time on Socrates embarked on the career of questioning for which he is famous, his object being to prove the oracle wrong. He thought, he said, that this would be an easy task, because he was only too well aware that he knew absolutely nothing. All he needed to find, it seemed, was somebody who knew something. This meant, then, that he tackled various 'wise' men on the subjects on which they were supposed to be expert. He did this in apparent innocence, only wanting to make sure that they really were wiser than he was himself, but this method of questioning quickly reduced them to confusion. As a result of this procedure two things happened: one was that Socrates finally decided that the oracle was probably right, in that although he knew nothing, he was wiser than the professedly wise, since he knew that he knew nothing, whereas they laboured under the false impression that they knew something. The second result was to be expected: Socrates became less and less popular with people of importance in Athens, and in 399 BC the two charges of introducing new deities and corrupting youth were brought against him. At his trial, Socrates made a reasoned defence of his way of life instead of making the usual impassioned appeal to the emotions of his judges, and was found guilty and sentenced to death. Ignoring the pleas of, among others, Plato, that he should attempt to escape, he drank hemlock and died.

THE DIALECTICAL METHOD

Apart from the powerful influence of this event on Plato as a young man, little is known of his life before the age of sixty. He was born in 427 BC, and probably his original ambitions were for public life or politics. Instead, his major contribution to the contemporary life of Athens, lay in his founding of the Academy, a fixed seat of learning, fulfilling the functions of a university where previously higher education had meant merely private contact with a foreign travelling teacher, a Sophist. Taylor guesses at a possible date for the founding of the Academy as 388–7 BC.[1]

At the age of sixty (367 BC) Plato became responsible for the education of Dion, the brother-in-law of Dionysius II of Syracuse. This gave him an opportunity to put into practice his ideas on the education of kings, but the experiment failed and Dion was banished from Syracuse. Another later attempt was also a failure.

Apart from these major events, what is to be known about Plato must be deduced from the dialogues (and letters) that he wrote.

In earlier dialogues the method of discussion, which is clearly a faithful representation of Socrates' methods, is dialectical. The DIALECTICAL METHOD is characterised by the fact that, at the outset, the aim is usually a definition, e.g. of justice, courage or beauty. A hypothetical definition is then suggested which should cover all cases; next a counter-example is found, and the definition has to be amended to cover this counter-example. The new definition is corrected and improved in the same way, and provides yet another definition, each definition being nearer to the truth than the last. The positive function of the dialectical method is, first of all, the clarification of ideas; secondly, the philosophical or logical training of those engaged in it; and thirdly, the examination of presuppositions. For instance, in mathematics, it is not enough to know *how* to square – you must understand the principle of it.

The earlier books of the *Republic*, the dialogue in which Plato puts forward the best-known of his educational ideas, begins by following this dialectical pattern, with the question, 'What is justice?' as the central theme. As the dialogue continues, however, discussion is gradually replaced by exposition, and instead of mere refutation of false notions of justice, a positive view is put forward, with full detail. For it emerges that Plato (through his spokesman, Socrates) believes that justice is something that can only be achieved in a certain sort of state. The rest of the *Republic*, then, consists in a description of this ideal state.

The most important feature of the state Plato describes is its division into three classes: first of all, the Guardians, who rule the city and are highly trained philosophers; secondly, the Auxiliaries, a military class for the defence of the city, but from whom the Guardians are recruited, and thirdly, the great mass of the population employed in business, the arts or manual labour. A great deal of attention is paid to the life of the Guardians, since the welfare of the city really depends on them, and Plato goes into the subject of their education and training in considerable detail. He also specifies that they shall lead a particularly disciplined existence, based on communistic principles. They shall not be allowed to possess houses or property of any kind; they shall take all their meals together. They are to be mated at occasional festivals and produce children, but there will be no permanent marriage and no one will know which are his or her children. Instead, the children are to be brought up in nurseries, and their mothers will be left free to play an equal part with the men in the government of the state.

This extremely controversial picture has been differently interpreted by different commentators. Some people have thought of the Guardians as a kind of Christian brotherhood, living according to the most liberal and humane principles; this was particularly true of earlier commentators on Plato. Others, and this is a much more recent view, have regarded Plato's ideal state as an inhuman dictatorial system, overshadowed only by the actual totalitarian régimes of recent times which, it is claimed, are indirectly based on it. This is the type of view that Karl Popper puts forward in *The Open Society and its Enemies*.[2] Which of these two viewpoints is nearer to the truth is not, however, a question that needs to be answered in order to consider the educational ideas that emerge in connection with the training of the Guardians.

It is important to realise that the education of the Guardians is, in the *Republic*, a matter that arises only incidentally in relation to the much larger question of the definition of justice. The description of the ideal state is, in fact, presented as Plato's answer to the question, 'What is justice?'. For Socrates suggests that, in order to find the answer, it will be necessary to consider what justice is on a large scale, i.e. in the state, before going on to the question of justice in miniature, or on a small scale, i.e. in the individual.

It is assumed that four main virtues may be found in the state: wisdom, courage, discipline (sōphrosynē – often translated as temperance) and justice. Socrates assumes that these are not only to be found in the state as a whole, but also in particular parts of the state. Agreement is reached that the first three virtues belong to the three parts of society in the following relationship:

1. Wisdom is the particular virtue of the Guardians.
2. Courage is the particular virtue of the Auxiliaries.
3. Temperance or discipline is a virtue of the state as a whole, which is displayed when there is a harmonious relationship between rulers and ruled.

Like temperance, justice does not belong exclusively to any one part of the state, but is to be found partly in the relations of the three with each other, partly in the attitude of each individual to the place, and more particularly the group, in which he finds himself. Justice consists, then, in each man fulfilling his particular function in society, and doing the job for which he is fitted.

But this description has been for purposes of analogy; between the state and that with which it is to be compared, the human soul, Plato draws some very exact parallels. To the three parts of the state correspond three parts of the soul.

1. To the Guardians or Rulers corresponds the reasoning part of the soul.
2. To the Auxiliaries corresponds the spirited part of the soul, i.e. the part of the soul which manifests itself in anger, indignation, courage, etc.
3. To the productive part of the state, the craftsmen, farmers, etc., corresponds the desiring part of the soul, conceived of by Plato as responsible for feelings of desire, such as thirst, or hunger, which are almost wholly physical.

The virtues in the soul follow the same pattern as the virtues in the state: wisdom is the virtue of the reasoning part of the soul and courage the virtue of the spirited part of the soul. Temperance again belongs to no one part, but consists in the harmonious working of all three parts of the soul. A soul is temperate, or disciplined, if that part of the soul which should command, i.e. the reason, does command, and if that part of the soul which should obey, i.e. the desiring part, does obey. Justice in this case consists in each part of the soul fulfilling its true function, or doing its job properly.

It is not entirely clear from this part of the *Republic* whether Plato considers that the desires or passions have any legitimate part to play in the life of the soul, or, to use the phrase suggested earlier, in a well-balanced personality. But the definitely inferior position assigned to them suggests an ascetic viewpoint, and this is confirmed in abundant references elsewhere (notably *Phaedo* 82C, et seq.) where the body and its desires are described as an encumbrance to the philosopher, who would do without them if he could, and will ignore them as far as he is able. In view of the analogy, this is an important point as regards the position of the productive classes in the state. One wonders if these too are to be regarded as a necessary evil, neither themselves nor their achievements having any intrinsic value. One wonders, too, whether, if the human personality exists for the

c

sake, and not for the fulfilment of its more physical desires, the state is to be thought of as existing for the sake of its philosopher-rulers, and not for the general satisfaction of the productive classes. That Plato would not have wished this sort of conclusion to be drawn is, however, clear from the emphasis he places both on the mutual benefits that will be derived from the threefold organisation of the state, and also on the willing consent of all the members.

But an essential consequence of the analogy is that the just life, in the commonly accepted meaning of the term, is a symptom of the just soul, in Plato's sense. And a just soul in this sense means a perfectly balanced personality. Plato's argument is that just as bodily health is considered a prerequisite for happiness, so should mental health be so considered. The Guardians are the people in Plato's state who should display this sort of justice, and a detailed description is given of the way in which their prolonged education will lead to this.

It has frequently been said that the education Plato recommends is a combination of the best features of the two vastly differing types of education of which Plato was aware in his contemporary scene: the Athenian, which was predominantly intellectual and cultural; and the Spartan, which emphasised demanding physical training and self-discipline with military success virtually the only recognised goal.

Plato stresses the importance of both these elements from the earliest stages, so following the pattern already established in Athenian education, where the broad description Music (musikē) covered the mental disciplines, and Gymnastic (gymnastikē) the training of the body. Music, a term which applied to literature and the arts generally, as well as to music in its narrower sense, is the first discussed. What is taught under this heading is considered by Plato to need very careful examination and selection. Some kinds of music (in the narrow sense) he considers can be 'effeminate' and weakening in their effect; therefore, he advocates that children in a state which must defend itself should be taught only stirring martial music, which will inspire rather than soothe them.

Where literature is concerned, Plato advocates an even more

strict and careful censorship. The stories with which Athenian children were familiar from an early age, occupied for them a similar place to the fairy-stories which form part of our tradition, but they also fulfilled the same kind of functions as the Bible stories which are, in most of our schools, the background to moral education. It was for this latter purpose that Plato found Athenian literature peculiarly unsuited. Traditional stories depicted both the gods and heroes as scheming, deceitful, adulterous and murderous. Many of the stories were, of course, allegorical but Plato argues:

A child is not able to discriminate between what is allegorical and what is not; on the contrary, the outlook he absorbs at that age tends to be indelible and unalterable – which is perhaps why at all costs we should see to it that the first stories he hears should have been framed with the best possible moral bias. (*Rep.* II 378)

Plato considers that the censorship he is recommending is not perverting the truth, but on the contrary supplying an essential truth of meaning, where otherwise a false picture might be given. This applies first of all to the actual facts that they suggest, for instance, about the corrupt nature of the gods; Plato argues that on the contrary goodness, not corruption, is an essential aspect of divinity. ('. . . We will have to look for other explanations of evil.' Ibid.) The other sense in which the stories are false relates to the type of moral training they supply. The Guardians must be brought up to think it disgraceful to quarrel with each other. Therefore, 'If we can manage to persuade them that no citizen ever quarrelled with another, and that this would be wrong, then this is what in the early years children should hear from the old men and women, and in adolescence from the poets.' (Rep. II 378.)

Death, again, must not be depicted as a terrifying and unpleasant future existence, since the state will need people who are not afraid to die.

This topic opens up a vast area for discussion and empirical research. Contemporary discussion centres on the question, not so much of oral story-telling, which was the only possible medium in Athens, but on the influence of cinema, television and comics on children and young people. Looked at in these terms, it will be seen that whereas the censoring of Greek myths may seem an unnecessary and repugnant notion, the principle that Plato is putting forward has, in fact, many contemporary supporters. In order to determine its validity, it would be necessary to conduct empirical investigations into the way in which films, stories, etc. (depicting for instance, violence) affect children. Such investigations have been conducted in both America and the United Kingdom and tend to show that some of these influences can be traced.[3] This, of course, does not provide a final answer to the question of whether Plato (or our contemporaries) are right to recommend such censorship, since there are people who hold that all censorship is wrong, for any age-group. Short of this extreme position, however, it is likely that evidence of significant antisocial effects would convince most people of the need for some kind of control in this area.

But Plato is interested in education not just to avoid antisocial behaviour, but to achieve a particular ideal stereotype; and it is at this point that his recommendations would part company with those of many liberal thinkers, for whom education is a matter of equipping pupils intellectually to make their own choices about the sort of lives they wish to lead, and the sort of values they will consider worth following.

Turning to the second aspect of early education in the *Republic* – Gymnastic – it appears that the purpose and point of physical education is, in Plato's view, military rather than either athletic, or, as modern educationists would see it, an end in itself. The emphasis on military training is dictated by the political set-up of the time – a continuous mainland inhabited by intermittently warring city-states. A novel feature of Plato's suggestions here was the equal inclusion of women as soldiers, and the attendance of children on the battle-field, partly for the help that older children might be able to give, but mainly as a part of their education. But this highly specific training is deferred to late adolescence, from eighteen to twenty; in the earlier stages of education, and for the younger child, the purpose or aim of physical training is not yet military, except in the sense that it should foster the military virtue of courage.

Instead, it is expected to contribute to the general education of the mind in the particular aspect which early education is designed to develop: the love of beauty. But whereas the literary/musical training achieved this intellectually, physical training aims at the same end through the emotions.

In Plato's general theory, an awareness of beauty is merely a step on a route which has as its final point, for a distinguished few, knowledge of goodness itself. This seems to be a quasi-religious experience, described in the *Republic*, as knowledge of the *Form of the Good*. The next stage of education is an intermediate point between these two experiences, knowledge of beauty and knowledge of the Good: *knowledge of truth*. The nearest manifestation of truth in this absolute sense is, on Plato's view, mathematics.

But this study is to be reserved for those who, at about the age of twenty, have passed through rigorous selection procedures designed to establish both that nothing will deflect them from making the good of the community their highest consideration, and that they are proof against 'toil and pain' (*Rep.* III 413) on the one hand, and the temptations of pleasure on the other. These will become the Auxiliaries, from the ranks of whom further tests after further studies will select the Guardians, or philosopher-rulers.

But before leaving the question of young children, it is of interest to compare Plato's attitude with current trends. In the following passage, having talked about the need for curbing licence in children's games in order that they may grow into law-abiding citizens, he continues:

They discover for themselves all those seemingly petty conventions abandoned by their predecessors: things like the young maintaining a fitting silence in the presence of their elders, and giving place to them; looking after parents; even such things as the way their hair is cut, the clothes and shoes they wear and all the details of physical deportment. (*Rep.* IV 425)

Although Plato goes on to say that actual legislation on these matters is unnecessary, it is clear that the trend of his thinking is more in line with traditional ideas on the subject than with that of present-day advocates of the self-expression of the child.

This impression is confirmed in a further passage where Plato describes the degeneration of democracy into anarchy.

The father falls into the habit of aping the child, and the child the father. He is afraid of his sons, and they neither respect nor fear their parents in the quest for 'freedom' . . . In the same way, the teacher is afraid of his pupils and panders to them; while they rather despise both their teachers and their tutors. Altogether, the young copy their elders, and are argumentative and disobedient; while the old, for fear of seeming to be unpleasant and authoritarian, imitate the young, trying to fit in with them by displays of genial *bonhomie*. (*Rep*. VIII 562)

From this it is clear that attitudes to the young in Plato's Athens were much nearer to contemporary practice than the attitudes which he recommends in their place.

But to continue with the description of the ideal, rather than the actual state: the study of mathematics, which occupies a span of about ten years, up to the age of thirty, is first of all justified by its general utility, including its usefulness in the all-important art of war; although the objective is not this mundane day-to-day utility, but rather the fact that the reason is being trained in abstract study in a way which will lead on to the culminating study of the Good. This will not be a first introduction to mathematics. A short aside in Book VII 536 suggests that, on the contrary, the two strands of early education, Music and Gymnastics, will be supplemented by a third, which, however, would only be introduced through play. Plato says:

Logic and geometry, and all the studies which form an essential preliminary to dialectic, should be introduced in childhood; but they must not be presented to them as compulsory instruction, since there is something wrong with the notion of a free person learning under compulsion. Purely physical tasks performed under duress do no harm to the body, but what is learned under duress just does not stay in the mind. So do not try to keep children at their studies by force, but by making them seem like play. (*Rep*. VII 536)

This idea is elaborated in the *Laws*, but before considering it, it is worth pursuing the scheme of education described in the *Republic* to its conclusion.

After completing his mathematical studies the potential

philosopher-ruler would undertake five years' study of dialectic followed by fifteen years' experience of public service, and only then, at the age of fifty, would it be appropriate for him to experience knowledge of the Good, and finally become at the same time both a philosopher and a ruler. The quality of this experience is described in an analogy which appears in Book VII, where the world of ordinary experience is compared to a cave in which men watch a kind of shadow puppet-show. They assume that the things they can see are the measure of reality, and have no conception of the experience of someone who manages to escape for a time to the upper world, and see the sun and the objects which exist in the world of light. The whole process of education for the Guardians has been, following this metaphor, an ascent from the cave: a process of learning to cope with increasing degrees of logical abstraction, a leaving behind of the world of the senses, which is the world of the particular, in order to arrive at the world of the intellect, where the Form of the Good has the same kind of dominance over other Forms, as has the sun over the world of visible objects. It is acquaintance with this highest Form, or degree of abstraction, that can be the culmination of the kind of life and education Plato has described in the *Republic*.

THE LAWS

The outlook of the *Republic*, which it is generally agreed was written by Plato in middle life, is in marked contrast to that of the *Laws*, the work of Plato's old age.

Whereas the *Republic* presents an ideal or Utopian picture with interest focused on the ruling-class, and scant attention is paid to the difficulties which reality might engender, the *Laws* is a prosaic and enormously detailed account of a way of life and system of education which is consciously tied in with the likely responses of ordinary people. Every class is considered, even the problems of non-conformists and delinquents. As Lodge points the contrast: 'Attention is concentrated upon the endeavour to meet the needs, not of imaginary concepts (as in the *Republic*), but of classes of real, flesh-and-blood men, women and children.'[4] Talking about the task of the administrator in the *Laws*, Lodge continues: 'His task is to take the material, human and imperfect as it is, and already biased in many ways, and to devise for it a constitution which will find, for every class, and for almost every individual, a part to play, and play with advantage, in the new "model" community: with satisfaction to everyone concerned.'[5]

Instead of the entire period up to eighteen being treated in general terms as one educational phase, the stages of schooling, more or less as we see them today, are given separate consideration in the *Laws*. Indeed, even the early rearing of babies is treated from a general educational standpoint, where the guidance given is permissive and indulgent, in the sense that picking up in response to crying is recommended, and also carrying round.

Only in the nursery years, three to six, does the practice of punishment or correction appear, and here the provision is made that it shall not be repressive or degrading, but shall be of a kind that will enlist the co-operation of the child rather than alienating him.

The same principle applies in respect of the work that is introduced at this period: it should be conceived of only in terms of play which is originated by the children, rather than imposed on them by adults; and for this purpose, Plato recommends the organisation of supervised play-grounds.

Serious lessons only start at the age of six, when the sexes are segregated. The broad division which was described in the *Republic* applies here, where lessons are seen as catering more specifically than in the *Republic*, for the body (Gymnastic) or the mind (Music). A long passage is introduced here on the value of teaching children to be ambidextrous.

Plato's plans for children's education in the *Laws* is unusual for his time; not only did he suggest that there should be schools with salaried teachers, but he also argued for a principle that has only in the last century come to be accepted in Britain – that children's attendance at these schools should be compulsory, since, as he puts it: 'They are children of the State rather than of their parents.' (*Laws* VII 804). A further revolutionary aspect which is carried over from the *Republic*, and one which has not yet won complete acceptance in our own time, is that there is no need for the education of girls to be differentiated in any respect from that of boys, even if their ultimate role in life may differ. In particular, military training should be common to both.

Apart from the learning which is covered by Music and Gymnastic, there are the sciences of arithmetic, geometry and astronomy. These Plato thinks, should be studied in depth only by the specially able, although every child should have a working knowledge of their elementary aspects. This should be arrived at principally through play, and he lists various number-games, involving the sorting of concrete objects like apples or dishes into number-groups.

But it is not the particular details of Plato's educational theory, as he puts these forward in the *Laws* and in the *Republic*, that have maintained a continuing interest in his views. On the contrary, it is his – or Socrates' – practice rather than his theory which most lends itself to imitation.

This practical technique is demonstrated in detail in the dialogue the *Meno*, where Socrates is represented as leading a completely illiterate and uneducated boy-slave to a recognition of the complex fact that a square with double the area of a given square can always be constructed on the diagonal of that square. Socrates achieves this solely by the use of leading questions, at no point handing over information to the boy which he must simply accept. The boy is encouraged to make reasonable guesses and follow out their implications until he sees for himself that they are wrong. Only after he has made several efforts of this sort to solve the problem himself does Socrates guide him to the correct solution with rather more directly leading questions.

In this incident Plato's best notions are portrayed, and concrete meaning given to his rather metaphysical statement in the *Republic* that the object of education must be the personal insight of the recipient rather than any ability for mere rote repetition. This is the implication of the passage in *Rep.* VII 518C which contrasts those educationists who think they can simply pour knowledge into the mind 'like sight into blind eyes', with Plato's own view of learning as following an innate capacity in the right direction.

That this is Plato's educational presupposition is, in fact, evident from the entire structure of the dialogues; and what G. C. Field says of Plato's view of philosophical knowledge can equally well be applied to his view of knowledge and learning generally.

True philosophical knowledge cannot be simply transmitted by one person to another. It can only be grasped by each person for himself after unstinted argument and counter-argument and question and answer.

SUMMARY

Plato held that virtue and knowledge were identical, both involving acquaintance with the world of Forms (abstract ideas), and both being necessary for happiness. Happiness, and therefore virtue and knowledge, could best be achieved, Plato held, in the kind of political organisation he describes in the *Republic*, and by people educated in the way he describes there.

The most striking feature of the organisation of Plato's ideal state is its division into three classes: the Guardians (ruler-philosophers), the Auxiliaries (the military class) and the productive classes – a structure which Plato finds paralleled in the structure of the individual personality, i.e. reason, emotion and the desires.

The protracted education of the Guardians combined cultural and intellectual development with physical and military training; it took place in the context of a communistic social system in which ordinary family life was abandoned, and women and men participated on equal terms. The broad general education which occupies most of the potential Guardian's childhood gives place to more specific military training from eighteen to twenty, and then to intensive and advanced mathematical studies for the years from twenty to thirty. After this, five years of dialectic precede fifteen years of public service, with the culmination of education only being reached at the age of fifty, when as both a philosopher and a ruler, the person may acquire full knowledge and virtue.

The scheme of the *Republic* is not continued in the *Laws*, where education is not considered a lifetime's occupation but is regarded as particularly the task of the years up to eighteen. Plato divides these years into specific stages and recommends an education which involves literary and musical pursuits, physical education, arithmetic, geometry and astronomy.

Apart from these expositions of his educational theories, Plato included in the *Meno* a demonstration of the practical technique of teaching which Socrates employed: a question and answer method, which elicits information without ever offering it as such.

NOTES

1. Taylor (48), page 6.
2. Popper (38), Part 1: Plato.
3. See Lovell (28), pages 198–200.
4. Lodge (27), page 242.
5. Lodge (27), page 243.
6. Field (18), page 180.

Passages in the chapter translated by author.

FURTHER READING

A useful abbreviated version of the *Republic*, with passages selected specially for their educational interest, is that by Boyd (8). The full version translated by Cornford (11) is, however, strongly recommended. Other dialogues of particular relevance for the philosophy of education are Plato's *Laws* and *Meno*.

Two books about Plato's philosophy in general are Field (18) and Taylor (48), while Nettleship's classic (34), although first published in the last century, is still recommended as a commentary on the *Republic*. For a different (and hostile) contemporary view of Plato's *Republic*, see Popper (38).

Particularly valuable discussions of Plato's educational theory are Lodge (26) and Lodge (27), chapters 10–12.

4 Rousseau

Jean-Jacques Rousseau, like Plato, began his life in a small city-state, thought by some to be the nearest the modern world has come to repeating the social and political climate of ancient Athens. This city-state, Geneva, where Rousseau was born in 1712, appears to have had as much influence on his political ideas as Plato's Athens had on his.[1] There Rousseau received his education, first from his father and later from a tutor. His early career was dominated by a considerable interest in music, and among several occupations which he tried was that of a teacher of music, as well as tutoring in a general sense. But the turning-point of his life came when in 1750, at the age of thirty-eight, his *Discourse on the Arts and Sciences* won a prize awarded by the Academy of Dijon. It was after this that all the works for which he is famous were published: *La Nouvelle Heloise* in 1761, and in 1762, the *Social Contract*, and *Emile*, Rousseau's main educational work. Principally because of its viewpoint on religious teaching, *Emile* was publicly condemned and ordered to be destroyed, and Rousseau himself only managed to avoid arrest by flight – first to Neuchâtel, and subsequently to England, where the philosopher David Hume offered him protection. Later he returned to France, and in 1770 to Paris, where he finished his *Confessions*, and wrote the *Dialogues* and *Reveries*. He died in 1778.

As in the case of Plato, extra light is cast on Rousseau's educational theory by an initial understanding of his overall philosophical position, and in particular his general political theory.

In the *Social Contract*, Rousseau's political thought was summed up in his famous statement that if anyone refuses to obey the general will, he should be 'forced to be free'.[2] It was his great stress, as a political thinker, on liberty (which he could not see as anything less than everyone doing exactly what he wanted, i.e. obeying only self-made laws), that resulted in the end in a totalitarian conception of the state. He saw the state as reflecting the 'general will' of the entire community, which could be identified with no individual's particular will, but for the sake of which it was justifiable, he held, to coerce the particular will of any individual.

This paradoxical argument for both total liberty and total coercion has left Rousseau in a strange historical position. On the one hand, his thought is counted as one of the foundations of western liberal democracy, first of all because of its direct influence in instigating the French revolution of 1789; and secondly, as inspiring indirectly the American Declaration of Independence. But on the other hand, he is with equal accuracy regarded as being the thinker, though again mediated through others, from whom stemmed the totalitarian systems of government of the Communist world.[3]

THE 'EMILE'

This paradox is of interest here because it is paralleled by a precisely similar contradiction in Rousseau's educational thought. Looking only at the *Emile*, one receives the impression of an educational thinker whose ideas centre on the notion of a private education provided by the parent either directly or by the provision of a tutor – an education, moreover, based on the ideal of the development of the child as an individual, with the unfolding of his particular personality as the teacher's objective.

In other writings, however, and particularly in his *Considerations on the Government of Poland* (1773), Rousseau advocates a state education which has as its objective the production of the type of citizen who will best serve the needs of the state. Indeed, in an earlier article for the *Encyclopédie* 1755 (9), he appears to put a point of view in total contradiction to that of the *Emile*, when he says:

It cannot be left to individual man to be sole judge as to his duties. Still less should children's education be left to the ignorance and prejudice of their fathers . . . Public education, regulated by the state, under magistrates appointed by the supreme authority, is an essential condition of popular government.

Here again is the contrast between extreme individualism and the total state domination of the individual which is characteristic of totalitarianism. The subject of an Emile-type education would lack political consciousness altogether until a very late stage in his development, whereas the recipients of the type of state education recommended for the Poles would not be offered the full and free development of Emile. But to some extent this paradox can be resolved, when account is taken of the fact that the Polish tract included proposals on the whole range of government, so that an ideal state, however unrealistically, could be assumed in recommending a state education.

The *Emile*, on the other hand, is set in the context of France as it was in the eighteenth century, where all its aspects were considered by Rousseau to be so unsatisfactory that the best possible service he felt he could do for a child would be to protect him from its influence by seclusion in the country.

Just as Rousseau's political ideas for all their inconsistencies attracted many followers and were the germ of new political philosophies, so his educational thought is the starting-point of what was called the New Education, and has influenced all the important thinking on education since his day.

In order to isolate the factors which brought this about, one has to distinguish the basic principles on which Rousseau's practical recommendations were based from the practical recommendations themselves. The latter have very little application outside the particular time and place at which they were made; they are essentially culture-bound. The former can be seriously considered, even if they are not found ultimately acceptable - although they *have* in fact been uncritically accepted by many subsequent educational thinkers.

There is room for some disagreement as to which of Rousseau's recommendations can be discounted as not essentially based on principle. But it seems clear that the educational structure of the *Emile* - a single child and a single tutor for the whole of the child's life – is not an essential aspect of the education Rousseau is recommending, but is rather the form which he uses as a vehicle for his ideas. Instead of a straight-forward educational treatise, Rousseau chooses to present his ideas in the form of a novel describing the upbringing of a particular boy: Emile.

Stages of development

In telling this story it emerges that Rousseau thinks of the development of the child in terms of stages; and that he believes that education should be geared to the particular stage of development that the child has reached. In emphasising that one should start from the child, Rousseau is consciously setting him-self against the eighteenth century's traditional outlook in education. He says:

The wisest writers devote themselves to what a man ought to know, without asking what a child is capable of learning. They are always looking for the man in the child, without considering what he is before he becomes a man.[4]

A second and more important feature of this child-centred approach is that it presupposes the essential goodness and purity of the child's nature. The widely accepted religious doc-trine of original sin allowed educationists to assume that educa-tion in all its aspects, but particularly its moral aspect, was a matter of improving on a basically corrupt and ill-intentioned human nature – making the child fit to live in adult human society. Rousseau, and the child-centred theorists who have followed him, posed a root-and-branch challenge to this assump-tion. To Rousseau, it was society which was corrupt, and natural man – and particularly the natural child – whose inno-cence tended to be compromised by living in society.

A picture of the corrupt effect of society, and of the primeval innocence of man before the advent of civilisation is painted by Rousseau in his second Discourse, 'On the origin of inequality'. There, in conscious opposition to the British philosopher, Hobbes (who had seen society, at least as regards security, as a comparative advance on the chaos and anarchy of life without an ordered social structure), Rousseau pictured a 'noble savage' guided only by his own self-love and his natural compassion for his fellow human beings, inhabiting a world infinitely preferable to the civilised world which succeeded it. In fact, he invites his reader to 'Compare without partiality the state of the citizen with that of the savage, and trace out, if you can, how many inlets the former has opened to pain and death, besides those of his vices, his wants, and his misfortunes'.[5] The comparison is, on Rousseau's view, entirely unfavourable to the citizen. He undervalues, in other words, the greater wealth and variety of experience made possible by civilisation, and stresses its less desirable features. This veneration for Nature had a decisive influence on both Rousseau's social theory and also his educational theory.

In education, the consequence is that the functions and aims of education become negative rather than positive. The educationist must protect his charge from the taint of the outside world, confident that if he can avoid the error of training a child in the wrong direction, then the child will have a natural inclination to develop in the right direction. As Rousseau puts it: 'The education of the earliest years should be merely negative. It consists, not in teaching virtue or truth, but in preserving the heart from vice and from the spirit of error.'[6] From the *Emile*, it would appear that the education offered to a child, apart from this negative aspect, would also avoid being narrowly vocational. Instead, it would be a training for later life in the broadest possible sense, including the teaching of a trade, and training for family and public or social responsibilities. Emile, in other words, is equipped to be an individual, a member of a family unit, and a member of the wider political community of which his family will be a part.

But these facets of education are only to be introduced at carefully defined stages. Rousseau considers that incalculable harm is done by premature presentation of material to a child. If, for instance, moral considerations are introduced when the child is not mentally equipped to absorb them, then a purely verbal facility with moral truths is reached, which makes it impossible, Rousseau thinks, for the ideas to be given appropriate and serious consideration when the child reaches an age when he *could* have coped mentally with moral abstractions.

The emphasis on stages is a feature of Rousseau's thought later followed up experimentally by the present-day psychologist, Piaget, with the same stress on the importance of introducing material for learning only at the stage when the child is physically and psychologically able to cope with it. Piaget has supplied documented detail of these stages; what Rousseau had to offer was, of course, pure guesswork. In looking at these individual stages, it will be possible to see to what extent those guesses were right or wrong.

Basically, four stages are involved: the first two are *infancy* and *childhood*, and both of these are sensory stages. The former involves sensations only, whereas the latter also involves sense-judgements. The third stage is *early adolescence* (from twelve to fifteen years); this is the intellectual stage, where practical thinking occurs. Lastly, there is *later adolescence* (after fifteen years), the moral stage, where thinking can be abstract.

Infant stage

Rousseau's remarks on the infant stage (strictly, babyhood) are full of good sense in relation to the practices of his time. It is often pointed out that while he emphasised the importance of parental care in his writing, in his private life Rousseau left his own children to the care of an orphanage. But in spite of this, one cannot but agree with his outspoken attack on the prevalent practices of his time. Flaubert's novel, *Madame Bovary*, reveals to what extent it was taken for granted in France at this time that any reasonably well-to-do mother would dismiss her child at birth to the care of a wet-nurse. The child would be wrapped in totally constricting clothing and spend its early life, perhaps crying, but immobile in the squalid home of a poor woman with many other claims on her energy and attention.

Rousseau argues powerfully for the importance to the child of the mother's own care at this stage both for the child's physical and emotional well-being. He also argues against the

D

swaddling practice on the grounds that freedom, in a purely physical sense, is essential for healthy development. This belief applies in a slightly different way, at every stage of development. In babyhood, it is extended to include activity and experience since these follow from freedom of movement and are as essential for mental and emotional development as the latter is for physical development.

Plainly influenced by the empiricist view in philosophy (according to which all knowledge derives ultimately from sense-experience) and in particular by the philosopher Locke, Rousseau justifies his position in these terms:

He (the child) wants to touch and handle everything; do not check these movements which teach him invaluable lessons. Thus he learns to perceive the heat, cold, hardness, softness, weight, or lightness of bodies, to judge their size and shape and all their physical properties, by looking, feeling, listening, and above all, by comparing sight and touch, by judging with the eye what sensation they would cause to his hand.[7]

A number of other lines of guidance are laid down by Rousseau in this section. He points out the dangers of being over-considerate to a child, so allowing him an over-dominating position; but he also offers sensible advice on the avoidance of battles of will with young children, and the deliberate substitution of conflict with *things* for conflict with people.

At this stage he simply says:

When children experience resistance in things and never in the will of man, they do not become rebellious or passionate, and their health is better.[8]

It is in relation to the second stage, childhood, that the notion of the discipline of things is built into a full theory. Here, Rousseau argues strongly against moral training or moral education in the conventional sense. Abstract moral notions, he suggests are beyond the comprehension of a normal child before the age of twelve. On the other hand, there are moral points that can be made by the teacher and fully appreciated by the child if a more practical approach is used. For example, Rousseau suggests arranging a situation in which the child's carefully tended beans are dug up by the gardener in order to make a telling point about property. Similarly, bad behaviour can be left to have its own consequences, rather than resulting in punishment. For instance, the deliberately broken window in a child's bedroom need not be repaired immediately, but the child could be left to experience a few cold nights. Rousseau feels that the concept of obedience and duty can be avoided altogether in bringing up a child, and that the positive virtues, like generosity or kindness can be better encouraged by example than by words. The alternative which Locke had suggested, 'Reason with children', Rousseau dismisses as completely inappropriate to their age and mental capacities.

Moral education is an area in which there is much current interest. One generally accepted presupposition of modern thought would seem to be that moral education cannot be successfully embarked upon only in adolescence, and that while indoctrination is clearly to be avoided, moral principles must be introduced at a much earlier age than Rousseau envisages. Although Rousseau's pupil, Emile, may be limited in his frustrations to contact with things rather than people – apart from such carefully staged incidents as the one with the gardener – most children will have had to learn to adjust socially with peers and adults long before the secondary stage. It is true, however, that these principles of social adjustment will be better learned by practice than by precept, and that open instruction, if offered, should start from the problems of the child's world, rather than that of the adult.

In considering the curriculum Rousseau offers to his charge for the childhood years, it is essential to bear in mind the poverty of the curriculum then offered in ordinary schools, which was based principally on the study of the classical languages with some geometry, history and geography added.

It is easy at this point to misunderstand Rousseau. He appears to be saying: postpone indefinitely any teaching of reading or writing, and avoid altogether history, literature, geography and religion. The latter are all beyond the comprehension of the child and any learning that appears to take place will, therefore, be merely surface or rote learning and purely verbal. In fact, Rousseau says:

When I thus get rid of children's lessons, I get rid of the chief cause of their sorrows, namely their books. Reading is the curse of childhood, yet it is almost the only occupation you can find for children. Emile, at twelve years old, will hardly know what a book is.[9]

However, when Rousseau expands upon this, it is clear that what he is prepared to offer in place of the accepted curriculum is something more like the best practice in the primary school.

For instance, instead of direct methods of teaching reading, he suggests the provision of incentives – making the child aware of the *use* of the skill before attempting to impart its mechanics. Rousseau would, he says, arrange for Emile to receive notes inviting him to, for example, a trip on the river – an idea capable of indefinite variation even in an ordinary classroom situation, where directions for doing things, labels for objects, etc., all lead to the child appreciating the use of the written word.

Rousseau's strictures on the teaching of geography would also be generally accepted today. The only emphasis was on the recognition of places on the map of the world, and Rousseau says:

I maintain that after two years' work with the globe and cosmography, there is not a single ten-year-old child who could find his way from Paris to Saint Denis by the help of the rules he has learnt. I maintain that not one of these children could find his way by the map about the paths of his father's estate without getting lost.[10]

Following Rousseau's priorities, geography in the primary school often does start with geography of the locality, the position of the shops on the way to school, etc. History, also, is introduced through the child's interests and surroundings: the history of the school, the church or of the village as the point of departure, rather than the conquests of Alexander or the Punic wars. Tradition, however, dies hard, and project-methods have by no means entirely supplanted the pre-Rousseau curriculum in present-day schools.

The whole aim of this stage of education is summed up by Rousseau in these words:

Leave childhood to ripen in your children . . . Nature would have them children before they are men. If we try to invert this order we shall produce a forced fruit immature and flavourless, fruit which will be rotten before it is ripe . . . Childhood has its own ways of seeing, thinking, and feeling; nothing is more foolish than to try and substitute our ways.[11]

Because so little of conventional knowledge seemed to Rousseau appropriate for this phase, where he confesses the object is not to save time but to lose it (simply to wait, in other words, for greater maturity), a great deal of the sort of learning Rousseau considers important must be crowded into the next three years, the period from twelve to fifteen.

Early adolescence

The key to this stage is the utilisation of the child's natural curiosity. It can be assumed, Rousseau thinks, that a child educated so far in the manner he has suggested will now have interests of a much broader scope than those that he had at an earlier stage. He will no longer, for instance, be prepared to know the sun simply as an object, but will be eager to pursue cosmological studies in some depth. Nevertheless, the method used by the teacher must still start from sense-experience; in this particular case, from going to a vantage-point to gaze at the broad sweep of the horizon. This principle of using an expedition or some kind of concrete experience as a stimulus for theoretical studies is now widely accepted as effective.

The concrete experience, however, may be used in conjunction with other more standard methods. But Rousseau sees it as an alternative to something to which he strongly objects: exposition, either in books, or through the mouth of the teacher. He advocated instead what have since been called discovery or heuristic methods. Emile, he said, would be allowed to discover the solutions to his own questions himself, and his teacher would be in no hurry to correct his mistakes. Indeed, Rousseau even held that the instruments for his discoveries should be invented by the child himself, his microscope, for example, or telescope. It is at this point that the present-day reader must part company with Rousseau's ideas. For whereas it was just possible, though by no means likely, that an eighteenth-century child should by his own efforts bring himself up to date with eighteenth-century scientific knowledge and equipment, advances in all fields have made the vast array of twentieth-century knowledge quite beyond the scope of the discovery or inventiveness of the twentieth-century child. The teacher today must strike a balance between the greater value of knowledge which is discovered and the greater variety and content of knowledge which can be imparted.

But Rousseau's objective is not, in fact, the production of someone who knows certain things – a point he is concerned to emphasise – but rather of a particular kind of person. To the extent that he is concerned with passing on knowledge, it is a matter of imparting practical skills, the knowledge of the applied scientist or engineer rather than of the theoretician. This is why he gives such extraordinary prominence to Defoe's book, *Robinson Crusoe*, in the education of Emile. It is, says Rousseau, the first book Emile will read, and for a long time it will be his only book.

The type of person Rousseau aims to produce is one who has a considerable potentiality for understanding and for acquiring knowledge, together with many valuable personal qualities, such as, independence and judgement. He says: 'Emile knows little, but what he knows is really his own; he has no half-knowledge ... He is large-minded, not through knowledge, but through the power of acquiring it.'[12]

In line with this objective, Rousseau recommends avoiding all competition and rivalry with other children and, in its place, substituting by keeping records the desire in Emile to improve upon his own performance.

Items which do not yet feature on Emile's curriculum are history, metaphysics and morals, and, more surprisingly, anything with aesthetic implications, such as poetry or poetic language. 'The time has not come,' says Rousseau, 'for feeling or taste.' Whether it will come after the age of fifteen, not having come before, is something Rousseau does not discuss.

One important feature which is included, however, and one which would have been controversial in those days for the son of a wealthy man, is the learning of a trade.

Later adolescence

The trade is continued in the next phase, that of later adolescence. Apart from this element of continuity, however, there is a radical break at this point with the education that has gone before. Up to the age of fifteen every effort has been made to restrict Emile's vision to the world of things. From fifteen onwards, the emphasis is on the world of men and their relationships to each other. History at last comes into Rousseau's scheme of education, though with some interesting remarks on its essential subjectivity. Rousseau expresses a preference for the classical historians, and classical and other literature is at last to be read for its own sake. At the same time Emile makes his acquaintance with the worlds of poetry and the theatre.

His moral education takes a new turn, with matters of sex, previously deliberately kept from him, needing to be explained and guidance given in the field of the emotions. Again Rousseau stresses the superiority of concrete examples over purely verbal cautionings and warnings. Like any modern writer on the subject he recommends frank speech, avoidance of sermonising, and a willingness on the part of the teacher to listen uncensoriously to the adolescent's problems, and to discuss them with him.

This is also the time for the discussion of religion, which is yet another area where Rousseau feels the child needs to be protected from premature knowledge. In the guise of an account of his own instruction from a Savoyard priest Rousseau expounds a religious viewpoint which was the main cause of his enforced departure from France on the publication of the *Emile*. Society today would be much more tolerant of what is virtually a religion of optimism, couched in terms sufficiently vague to be acceptable to any religious body which avoids dogmas, creeds and outward forms of worship – for example, Quakers or Unitarians. Rousseau's ideas stem from consideration of the differences between the more highly formalised religions, and it is interesting to reflect that it is just these differences that have led in English state schools to a system of religious teaching which in its avoidance of dogma is not unlike that recommended by Rousseau.

Education of women

Consideration at this stage of the question of a wife for Emile leads Rousseau to make some observations on the subject of the education of women, and in particular of Sophie, the woman whom he destines for Emile. His observations here are not worth any detailed consideration, as they are as reactionary as his general views on education are revolutionary. Entirely mirroring eighteenth-century attitudes on the subject, he starts from the premiss that 'woman is made for man's delight . . . woman is made to please and to be in subjection to man.'[13] He therefore recommends the type of education that, in spite of his contempt for these institutions, combined the philosophy of the convent and the finishing school – the former type of education being directed to the production of the capable wife, the latter to the development of such graces as would ensure the young girl's *becoming* a wife.

Rousseau is fully aware of alternative attitudes, those of Plato, for example, and of some of his contemporaries who recommended a more solid basis for the education of women. Rousseau, however, remains convinced that 'The search for abstract and speculative truths, for principles and axioms in science, for all that tends to wide generalisation, is beyond a woman's grasp; their studies should be thoroughly practical. It is their business to apply the principles discovered by men, it is their place to make the observations which lead men to discover these principles.[14]

It has already been remarked that Rousseau dislikes the idea of books playing a large part in education. ('Let all the lessons of young people take the form of doing rather than talking; let them learn nothing from books which they can learn from experience.')[15] Where the education of women is concerned, this dislike is even more pronounced. Rousseau's ideal woman will have read only two books, and one of these will have come her way by chance.

It is not surprising that intelligent women of the period, particularly in England, were incensed by Rousseau's views. It is necessary to remember, though, that the principle of complete non-differentiation of boys' and girls' education, for which such famous pioneers of women's education as Emily Davies and Frances Mary Buss fought in England, is still controversial. Indeed, it is an ideal specifically denied in the Newsom Report in relation to the education of children of average and below-average ability. However, although it is possible to consider some concession to the principle of differentiation, it is unlikely that anyone now could consider such an extreme position as that put forward by Rousseau in the *Emile*.

But the digression does not mark the end of Rousseau's educational scheme for Emile. Before the marriage, Rousseau recommends two or three years of travel designed to equip him with a knowledge of politics and government, which will enable him to return ultimately to his own country with some understanding of what it is to be a citizen. No new educational principles emerge here, though, and this passage is a good deal less specific than the earlier ones.

CONCLUSION

This discussion has centred round the *Emile*. It should be mentioned, however, that many of Rousseau's educational ideas are also described in Part V of *La Nouvelle Heloise*. It is in the *Emile*, though, that these ideas are most systematically worked out.

One or two general criticisms arise out of the form in which Rousseau's ideas are presented in the *Emile*. Because Rousseau ties the child's education so closely to certain fixed stages of development, it is possible to argue, with some justification, that he is not as aware as he should be of growth as a continuous process, with changes taking place by imperceptible degrees, rather than in sudden leaps. This is linked with a further failing which most commentators have remarked upon: the fact that Rousseau assumes a faculty psychology. That is to say, he appears to believe that new faculties appear as a child reaches a new phase of development. In fact, of course, every adult ability has its less-developed forms at every level of childhood; the ability to make brilliant speeches, for instance, is not a totally new skill that belongs to adult life, but only the adult equivalent of the baby's babbling, or the child's simple sentence communication with its mother. And if Piaget's work appears to give some support to the notion of fixed stages of development, it must be remembered that Piaget's work is valid only as regards the order in which various mental skills and abilities appear, and not as regards actual ages, since tremendous variation is possible among children. Also, Piaget's work is empirical, and behaviouristic, so that what he claims to investigate is the order in which children *do* specific things, not in which they acquire special faculties.

However, it is not because of his emphasis on stages of growth that Rousseau revolutionised educational thinking. The ideas which made a lasting impact were, first of all, his recommendation of heuristic (discovery) methods, the learner-oriented approach which stemmed from his other main recommendation: that education should start from the needs of the child. And lastly, child-centred theorists have continued to share his view of the purpose of education, which is that the educator should aim at producing a particular type of person, rather than a person with any particular knowledge; in other words, that the aims of education should be therapeutic rather than purely academic or informative. The best-educated person is, on Rousseau's view, the one who can 'best endure the good and evil of life'.[16]

SUMMARY

Rousseau put forward his main educational ideas in the *Emile*, which is an account of a boy's education by his tutor. His development is presented in distinct stages, each introducing a new phase of education.

Rousseau maintains that the needs of the child as a child must determine the education that is offered, rather than the needs either of society or of the child in adult life. This implies permitting the child the maximum amount of freedom from direction and control, a policy which is justified for Rousseau by his faith in the natural goodness of unconstricted human nature. On Rousseau's view, it is society alone that corrupts.

The four stages of development which Rousseau discusses are infancy, childhood, early and later adolescence. He argues in favour of freedom at each of these stages, to permit of activity leading to experience and discovery. The emphasis is on manipulating concrete objects and dealing with real situations, rather than upon reaching intellectual knowledge solely through reading or through learning the correct responses to certain questions.

Up to the end of the first two stages, at the age of twelve, education is limited to the simpler elements of the child's immediate world. In the third stage, it is expected that his natural curiosity will lead him to discoveries in the world of science, and in the fourth stage, from fifteen to eighteen, to social and aesthetic studies, including history, literature, poetry and religion.

NOTES

1. See Rousseau, *Letter to d'Alembert*.
2. Rousseau (41), page 41.
3. See Talmon (46), Part 1, chapter III.
4. Rousseau (39), page 1.
5. Rousseau (41), page 224, Appendix.
6. Rousseau (39), page 57.
7. Rousseau (39), page 31.
8. Rousseau (39), page 33.
9. Rousseau (39), page 80.
10. Rousseau (39), page 74.
11. Rousseau (39), page 54.
12. Rousseau (39), page 169.
13. Rousseau (39), page 322.
14. Rousseau (39), page 349.
15. Rousseau (39), page 214.
16. Rousseau (39), page 9.

FURTHER READING

Direct reading of Rousseau's own writings is recommended: the *Social Contract* and *Discourses* (41) for his social and political theory, and the *Emile* (39) for his educational theory. His educational views are also presented in *Julie ou la Nouvelle Heloise* (40), Part V.

An abbreviated version of the *Emile*, with introductory notes and comments, is that by Boyd (6), who has also edited a selection of Rousseau's minor educational writings (9).

Other short discussions of Rousseau's educational ideas are to be found in Curtis and Boultwood (12) and Rusk (42).

5 Froebel

Friedrich Froebel's position in the history of educational thought
is a unique one. Although his principal ideas had already been
suggested in the writings of Rousseau, there were two ways in
which the world was forced to take notice of those ideas as
presented by Froebel, whereas it might have forgotten them had
only the influence of Rousseau been involved. In the first place,
Froebel was a teacher, and set up his own school incorporating
his ideas in practice. And secondly, as a direct result of this, his
ideas fired his followers with an almost evangelical and crusad-
ing fervour which took his ideas out of the academic world and
into the real world as a movement with international organisation and wealthy and influential backing.

As a movement, Froebelianism's day of glory passed in the
first decades of this century. In the hands of less perceptive
disciples and imitators, the practical applications of Froebel's
teaching became rigidified in a formal and didactic approach
which was the exact opposite of Froebel's broader aims. These
were taken up and developed in the work of John Dewey – a
development which merits separate treatment – but they continue to exert a living influence on contemporary educational
thinking and practice. This is partly because of the extent to
which education courses for teachers-in-training often unconsciously transmit and reflect his values and ideas; and this in
itself has its historical explanation in the contribution which
Froebel exponents have made to teacher-training.[1] While their
personal influence has diminished, their view of education remains embodied in the child-centred education syllabus of
many colleges, where prominence is given to child development,
and to the observation of children. As syllabuses are revised and

overhauled, it may be that even this influence will wane, and that education courses will come to reflect the scientific and materialist values of the later twentieth century; but it is doubtful whether classroom practice in the education of young children could ever shake itself free of the general patterns of Froebel-inspired instruction.

Froebel's greatest fame is as the originator of the KINDERGARTEN, although his educational interests were, in fact, more general than that. The name, kindergarten (garden of children), was a conscious expression of his basic educational outlook. He compared the child to a seedling plant, and the task of the teacher to that of the gardener, who has merely to provide the right environment for the plant to develop naturally to the best of its potential.

BACKGROUND

Before considering the wide implications of this analogy, it is necessary to look briefly at the personal background and experience which led Froebel to his final educational and philosophical position. He was born in Germany in 1782 at Oberweissbach, a village in the Thuringian forest. As a youth, he was apprenticed to a forester, and developed an interest in nature, which was later reflected strongly in his school curriculum. Following this apprenticeship, he joined his brother at Jena University where he was able, for a time, to develop his scientific and mathematical interests. Then followed a series of occupations including teaching and tutoring, and contact with other universities – Göttingen and Berlin, where he worked on crystallography. During this period, 1808–10, he was exposed to the major educational influence of Pestalozzi, at Pestalozzi's school at Yverdun. In the same way that Pestalozzi was influenced by Rousseau, although disagreeing with him on many points, so Froebel, although critical, was won over by Pestalozzi's approach.

War service intervened before Froebel was able to set up, in 1816, the school which was to be the vehicle of all his ideas. Although founded elsewhere, by the following year the school had its permanent site at Keilhau, in the Thuringian region of his birth. From this point on, Froebel began to produce his many articles and publications on education including, in 1826, *The Education of Man.*

Froebel's death, in 1852, took place in the shadow of a government ban (imposed the previous year) on kindergartens in Prussia – imposed, some commentators think, owing to a simple confusion of identity, which linked the movement with socialism. But despite this, Froebel's supporters, in particular the Baroness von Marenholtz, were already propagating his ideas on an international scale, and by the 1870s, there were kindergartens in France, Holland, Italy, England and America.

PHILOSOPHY

All Froebel's earlier experiences combined to produce in him his distinctive point of view. His varied, but admittedly unconventional and unsystematic university experience, led directly to his basic philosophical position. German philosophy of this period was heavily metaphysical in tone, and through Schelling, Froebel came under its influence. The direction of his researches in biology, mathematics and, in particular on the structure of crystals, led him to believe that there was one underlying structure in nature. It was a short step, in the shadow of Hegelian philosophy to move from this to a belief in a total underlying unity embracing man himself and his total environment, both material and immaterial. Because Froebel believed in the divine nature of this unity, this is a view which, although Christian in intent, is pantheistic in a somewhat similar way to the religious outlook of Rousseau. But whereas religion was compartmentalised in Rousseau's educational theory, Froebel's pantheistic philosophy pervaded all his recommendations for educational practice.

In the first place, it led directly to a demand for unity and continuity in the curriculum. (One of Froebel's criticisms of Pestalozzi was that the different parts of his curriculum were unrelated.) In addition, he refers elsewhere to the men at the universities 'who had divided the field of education into separate areas of knowledge and had provided us with a vast literature'.[2] The demand for the integrated curriculum, and opposition to 'narrow subject specialisms' is currently being felt at all educational levels, and it may be illuminating to see where, in the hands of less-inspired followers, this idea led at the nursery and primary level. O. B. Priestman, after specifying by contrast some of the valuable ways in which unity of theme can provide a basis for teaching, reports that 'It was possible to see children of six years begin the morning by singing a song about ducks; go on to do arithmetic about ducks, ducklings, duck eggs, etc.; study the "Ducks' Ditty" for poetry; copy out a verse of it for writing; model a duck's nest from plasticine (of all unsuitable media), and finish up with a story of the Ugly Duckling.'[3] But for a contemporary account of the integrated method successfully applied, though not in this case for any doctrinaire reasons, the reader may like to refer to Sybil Marshall's account of her own experience in *An Experiment in Education* (29). She describes, for instance, how a single piece of music led to a whole term's valid work in history, geography, art, literature, etc.

Unity of knowledge

But Froebel's scheme was based on the metaphysical notion that in some sense all human knowledge in the form of conventional subjects is an aspect of one single object. This is a notion which will have little appeal to the empirically-minded; it could, in fact, be termed mystical, rather than metaphysical, since it is a common feature of the teaching of mystics. Froebel, however, would not have regarded this as a criticism, since his own criticism of Pestalozzi was that he was too empirical in his approach – by which he meant that he took the ordinary world of facts and sense-perceived objects for granted.

From this starting-point Froebel went on to say that, unlike the rest of Nature, man could progress to consciousness of this one divine reality. He could do this by developing according to an inner principle, rather than one imposed externally by an educator or parent. It is here that the analogy with the plant appears. Froebel says:

To young plants and animals we give space and time, knowing that then they will grow correctly according to inherent law; we give them rest and avoid any violent interference such as disturbs healthy growth. But the human being is regarded as a piece of wax or a lump of clay which can be moulded into any shape we choose. Why is it that we close our minds to the lesson which Nature silently teaches?[4]

There are several implications here. First, as in the case of Rousseau, the widely accepted doctrine of original sin is implicitly repudiated. It was a belief in the natural tendency of the child to go wrong that led to the 'moulding' view of education. Froebel substitutes a faith in the natural goodness and innocence of childhood, and a belief that a permissive upbringing will result in a child developing of his own accord on the best possible lines. Specifically applying this conclusion to education, he says: 'Education must be permissive and following, guarding and protecting only; it should neither direct nor determine nor interfere.'[5]

This notion of freedom in education is one which will be more fully discussed in connection with modern trends, but there are one or two problems specifically connected with this particular formulation of the view.

First, Froebel takes a particular end-product for granted, without making it absolutely clear what type of child would count as one who had developed in the 'naturally right' way. We may understand the notion of a physically healthy child, by analogy with the healthy plant, but education is also concerned with the mind, and it is by no means certain that everyone could agree on what constituted a rightly-developed mind.

Secondly, freedom in a school can be taken to apply to behaviour and discipline; but probably freedom to behave as they chose was not something that Froebel intended to advocate for his pupils. Instead, it was freedom in a different sphere that he recommended: that of the curriculum. And here is the first contradiction in his thought. For Froebel believed that he could anticipate the choices that would be made by the naturally free child, and so devised a very carefully planned curriculum, which is what, earlier this century, came to be regarded as *the* Froebel system. This included the gifts, occupations, finger-plays

E

and singing games, which many teachers learned to use, some without understanding their significance, or their originator's intentions. (The 'gifts' were objects of mathematical significance – the sphere, the cylinder and other geometrical shapes, and they were introduced systematically, since Froebel believed that through playing freely with them, the child would gain an insight into the underlying structure of the world, and understand its basic unity.) As a result, the scope for genuinely free activity in Froebel schools was limited by the strongly teacher-guided activities which were intended to aid it.

Developmental stages

The self -activity of the child will be considered in more detail later. Still, for the moment, considering the plant analogy, a second implication of this comparison was an emphasis on developmental stages. Froebel recognised as discrete stages *infancy, childhood, adolescence* and *maturity*, and, like Rousseau, he held that each stage should be fully exploited and enjoyed in its own right (i.e. not for the sake of the next or the mature stage). Nevertheless, there is, Froebel thought, an ultimate goal for all development, which is the consciousness or awareness mentioned earlier. This again is linked with his basic metaphysical viewpoint, in that he holds that the stages of development through which the child passes are a reflection of the stages of development of human society; and just as the child, the microcosm, tends through these stages to an optimum, so Froebel believes that society, the macrocosm, is tending through *its* various stages to its optimum. The philosophy, then, is one of human goodness, progress and perfectibility – a faith which, unfortunately, human history since Froebel's lifetime, has done much to undermine.

Froebel considers it essential for the educator to ensure that the intellectual, emotional and physical needs of the child are fulfilled at each stage. 'Satisfactory development,' says Froebel, 'at any one period can be achieved only if there has been fulfilment at the earlier levels of growth.'[6] It is this belief that has led to the stress on the study of child development in teacher-training courses, since, if this belief is accepted, it becomes essential for the teacher to understand fully the needs and characteristics of each phase.

Again, though, there is room for disagreement as to what are the needs and characteristics of each phase. Priestman revealingly comments: 'It is for this reason that the Froebel teacher is often hard pressed to stop an over-ambitious parent from hurrying a child too fast through his natural stages of growth.'[7] The complaint of parents, on the other hand, is that this type of education unduly delays the acquisition of the basic skills of reading, writing and number; as well as, at later stages, acquaintance with the adult worlds of art, literature and science.

As in the case of Rousseau, we can see that Froebel's viewpoint was against the over-valuing of intellectual skills, and in favour of much greater emphasis on practical skills and on social and inter-personal development: for the young child, things rather than books. S. J. Curtis and M. E. A. Boultwood (12) quote an American satire on the Froebelian type of education which aptly illustrates this fundamental difference of opinion as to what is of *value* on the teaching time-table.

They taught him how to hemstitch, and they taught him how to sing,
And how to make a basket out of variegated string.
And how to fold a paper so he wouldn't hurt his thumb;
They taught a lot to Bertie – but he couldn't do a sum.
They taught him how to mould the head of Hercules in clay,
And how to tell the difference 'twixt the blue bird and the jay,
And how to sketch a horsie in a little picture frame,
But, strangely, they forgot to teach him how to spell his name.

Originally quoted in *Pestalozzi and Froebel* by F. H. Holland (1904).

Although this may be taken to describe the excesses rather than the norm, it should be appreciated that even taken at face value, the New Education was a healthy reaction against the excessive formality and rigid teaching of more conventional skills which prevailed at the time. However, what Piaget's further work on developmental stages has shown is that there was some truth in both points of view. On the one hand, it is now accepted as a result of much empirical research that different aptitudes appear at different and recognisable stages of development, and that the attempt to impart them earlier literally cannot meet with success. But it is also accepted, as a valid criticism of Piaget's own earlier assumptions, that these developmental stages cannot be tied rigidly to chronological ages. The parent, for instance, who considers his child ready to read before six may, after all, be right as regards *his* child. Froebel's developmental theories, then, although vastly over-simplified when compared with Piaget's recent and detailed researches, have the same strengths and weaknesses as these later developmental views.

Play

Allied to this difference of emphasis in the curriculum was another principle of Froebel's which was open to considerable misunderstanding and misinterpretation. This was a belief in the value of children's play for learning and development. Froebel claims:

Play is the highest level of child development. It is the spontaneous expression of thought and feeling – an expression which his inner life requires. This is the meaning of the word 'play'.[8]

Froebel goes on to to say that the child takes his play seriously; for him, play is work. For the supervising adult, the child's play is even more significant, for through his play the child develops his personal qualities for adult life. Froebel claims that in play the foundations of this later life are laid down; in particular: 'whether it shall be rich or poor in achievement, and whether he will be gentle or violent, show apathy or intelligent insight, create or destroy'.[9]

Play, in other words, is self-expression. Froebel was well aware of it as a contrast to productive work, though not to ordinary aspects of the school curriculum. He attached a different, but positive, value to productive work, and even recommended that the child should be expected to engage in it for one or two hours each day; gardening was particularly favoured from this point of view. Nevertheless, the emphasis on play was frowned upon by a generation that had a total respect for the notion of work. As Froebel himself commented, they tended to regard even the carefully planned 'gifts' of the Froebel system as a waste of time. In addition, once the Montessori system became generally known and established, it provided a practical contrast to Froebel's 'Play Way', since Montessori held that the child shares an adult's attitude to work and play, and wants the importance attached to serious work.

Self-activity

The Montessori system posed a further challenge to that of Froebel, as the two systems ran parallel for a time in the first decades of the present century. Montessori replaced teacher-guidance entirely with apparatus designed to carry the child along at his own pace and according to his own wishes (one of the principles of modern programmed learning). But as has already been observed, while Froebel set a high value on the self-activity of the child, the system he devised actually contained considerable scope for teacher-guidance, group activities and collective or whole-class activities – stories, songs and games. Nevertheless, it should not be thought that Froebel was paying lip-service only to his own principle, and it should be noted that it is something like his balance between self-direction and teacher-direction that is practised in most infant schools today.

The reason for setting a high value on the activity of the child rather than on the part the teacher had to play, was a belief in the efficacy of learning by one's own achievements – learning by doing – rather than simply receiving information. Learning, in other words, is an active rather than a passive process, at least in the case of the young child; and Froebel emphasised the position of the child as a doer, rather than as a recipient of facts. Commenting on his own background, Froebel says:

My experiences, especially those of my university career, had taught me quite unequivocally that existing educational methods, especially if mere instruction or the communication of external facts and historical explanations was the aim, blunted – I might even say destroyed –

any attempt in the schools to promote true knowledge or give any genuine scientific training.[10]

A genuine scientific training was, in fact, something that the Froebel schools particularly tried to offer, but starting as such instruction would today, from the children's own discoveries and interests. Nature study had a much larger share of the time-table than it would be likely to have now, but it had considerable scope, frequently including a walk and taking in activities which would now be termed 'environmental studies.'

Self-activity, then, was valued as an aid to learning – the shop, for instance, with its money, weights and measures, replacing sum-cards in arithmetic. It was also valued as a means of encouraging creativity. Creativity is clearly regarded as a form of play, and hence of self-expression, but it is a distinctive form of play, and, though Froebel does not necessarily distinguish them, the two notions do not exactly overlap. In fact, creativity itself was often used as an aid to learning, with painting, modelling, etc., immediately following upon, and intended to express, some piece of presented learning. But there can be little doubt that creativity was considered by Froebel to have an intrinsic value in relation to the child's personal development, in the same way as other more generalised forms of self-expression. The equal value of these differing aspects is made clear by Froebel in the *Pedagogics of the Kindergarten*, where he describes the type of school he favours. It will achieve its ends, he says, 'by encouraging the child's impulse to activity, investigation and creative work. It will be an institution where children instruct and educate themselves and where they develop and integrate all their abilities through play, which is creative self-activity and spontaneous self-instruction.'[11]

One minor aspect of Froebel's teaching, which again reflects Rousseau's ideas, is his opposition to the encouragement of any form of competition between children. Children, he thought, have a natural urge to do the best they can, given encouragement. It is not certain, however, whether the Froebel system manages to avoid the incentives of reward and punishment altogether, or whether it simply replaces an open system of marks with a more intimate and personal system of gradations of approval and disapproval on the part of the teacher. To some extent, though, this system achieves its objective of deflecting children's attention from comparisons with each other's performance.

Criticisms

Some criticisms of Froebel's theories and ideas have already been discussed but there are some more general criticisms that deserve mention. The first major criticisms of Froebel were made in a lecture by Professor Graham Wallas who argued that Froebel's evolutionary theories (pre-dating, as they did, those of Darwin) totally undervalued the effects of environment on development, with their view of change and development proceeding from within the child or species.[12] This is an important criticism, since Froebel's whole emphasis on freedom and self-activity depends upon his belief in the possibility of this natural development. This criticism, with its sociological implications, is underlined, too, by Nathan Isaacs, who points out that Froebel not only undervalues the effects of social environment on the child, but also overlooks the necessity for the child himself to be trained to fit in with the society he is to join.[13]

Further criticisms stem from the fact that Froebel lived in an era which preceded the development of modern experimental psychology. Hence his child psychology can be stigmatised as insufficient and in part erroneous. Isaacs points out, for instance, that Froebel seems unaware of the possibility of any real differences between children. They all tend to the same stereotype, Man, and the education Froebel offers them is limited in variety and the same for all. Modern psychological investigations have established beyond question that children are born with different inherent abilities and even with different leanings and skill potentials. (For instance, creativity itself seems to be a quality possessed by certain children and these may be children who do badly on conventional IQ tests.) In Froebel's terminology, then, we would say that children have different innate capacities for growth. This is not, however, something that could easily have been recognised in an era of poor and limited education and pre-scientific psychology.

Finally, it must be admitted that in terms of social and political ideas, Froebel was not as progressive as in his educational theory. There is, for instance, an emphasis on the education of boys and a feudal attitude to servants; and although extremely concerned for the education of the poor, Froebel justified it with this comment: 'There need be no fear that individual pupils will want to improve their position and leave their own class.'[14]

He added that the socially-ambitious poor could always enter the teaching profession!

Conclusion

However, Froebel is to be judged not primarily as a social thinker, nor even as a psychologist, but for the contribution he made to the field of practical education. And here the tribute paid to him by W. N. Hailmann in his early introduction to Froebel's *The Education of Man* (21) is still probably a fair assessment.

Perhaps the greatest merit of Froebel's system is to be found in the fact that it furnishes a deep philosophy for the teachers. Most pedagogic work furnishes only a code of management for the schoolroom.

Whatever the inadequacies of the philosophical base, its effect was certainly to encourage a much deeper and more thought-out approach to the task of practical teaching.

SUMMARY

Froebel's educational ideas were propagated through the Froebel movement and exemplified during his lifetime in his own school.

They stemmed from a basic metaphysical belief in an underlying unity beneath the apparent variety and differentiation of the world and of human experience. This belief led Froebel to recommend an integrated approach to the curriculum, exploiting links between subjects wherever possible.

He compared the development of the child to that of a plant, implying that unhampered natural development would produce the best possible results, and recommended a maximum amount of freedom in education. However, he himself constructed a detailed and specific educational system, which involved much teacher-guidance.

Froebel held that the child's development could be divided into the four stages of infancy, childhood, adolescence and maturity. He maintained that each stage had its own needs, which had to be fulfilled *at that stage* for successful progress to be made to the next stage.

Play was held by Froebel to be one of these basic needs, and also to be a significant preparation for adult life. Froebel set a high value on encouraging the child's own activity, his scientific interests, and his creativity.

NOTES

1. See 'History of Froebel Movement' in Lawrence (23).
2. Lilley (25), page 35.
3. Lawrence (23), page 147.
4. Lilley (25), page 52.
5. Lilley (25), page 51.
6. Lilley (25), page 64.
7. Lawrence (23), page 142.
8. Lilley (25), page 83.
9. Lilley (25), page 84.
10. Lilley (25), page 41.
11. Lilley (25), page 92.
12. Lawrence (23), page 87.
13. Lawrence (23), page 182.
14. Lilley (25), page 164.

FURTHER READING

Translations of Froebel's works dating from before the turn of the century are Hailmann (21) (*The Education of Man*), Jarvis (22) (*Pedagogics of the Kindergarten*) and Michaelis and Moore (31) (Froebel's autobiography).

It is recommended, however, that a selection from Froebel's writings in a modern translation be studied in preference to these, at least to begin with, in particular Lilley (25).

In order to gain an understanding of the Froebel movement and of the wider implications of Froebel's teaching, read Lawrence (23), which includes contributions from different authors on a variety of aspects of Froebelianism.

6 Dewey

It is in connection with Dewey that the term 'the progressive school' was first used to sum up the trend in education which started with Rousseau and was followed through in the work of Pestalozzi, Froebel and, at the beginning of this century, Dewey himself. John Dewey was born in 1859 in Vermont, USA, and died in 1952. Into that life-span of nearly a century, Dewey crowded what could have been the distinguished achievements of several different lifetimes. His interests were wide-ranging, and he achieved recognition by philosophers as a philosopher and by educationists as an educator and educational theorist. In both these fields his output of books and articles was prodigious.

1859, the year in which Dewey was born, was, as William Brickman points out[1] the year in which Charles Darwin's *Origin of Species* was published, as well as Karl Marx's *Critique of Political Economy* and John Stuart Mill's *On Liberty*: three works which played an enormous part in shaping the history of the ensuing century. The first because it revolutionised man's view of man; the two latter because they represent the rival ideologies of communism and liberalism. After college and two years' teaching experience, Dewey undertook two years (1882–4) of study at the John Hopkins University in Baltimore leading to the degree of Doctor of Philosophy. Following this he taught at the Universities of Michigan and Minnesota, and from 1894 to 1904 he was Chairman of the Department of Philosophy, Psychology and Pedagogy at the University of Chicago (on the basis of a reputation already established by books in these various fields). Here for seven years, he and his wife ran a laboratory school, linking educational theory directly with educational practice. The story of his departure from this post is an interesting one, reflecting as it does Dewey's lesser degree of success in the area of administration and personal relationships.[2] From 1904 until his retirement in 1930, Dewey was Professor of Philosophy at Columbia University, New York, at the same time teaching the philosophy of education at the Columbia Teachers' College.

EDUCATIONAL THEORY

It is difficult to select what is most representative from Dewey's many writings. From the point of view of educational theory, however, Dewey's most important work was undoubtedly *Democracy and Education* (14), first published in 1916, and it is interesting and illuminating to consider this in relation to a book he published in collaboration with his daughter, Evelyn, the year before, *Schools of Tomorrow* (17); in addition to linking his ideas directly to those of earlier educators, the earlier book provides practical descriptions of what went on during the school day in schools which adopted his methods or similar ones. Both, however, have to be considered in the light of *Experience and Education* (15), in which twenty years later Dewey criticised the abuses of progressivism which had gained ground since those early days.

Dewey's basic philosophical position, which he called INSTRUMENTALISM, was a development of American PRAGMATISM – a philosophical theory whose principle exponents were C. S. Peirce and William James – both contemporaries of Dewey.

Pragmatism is a view concerning the nature of truth, and consequently of knowledge. The pragmatist holds that there is no absolute truth, but claims that to claim that something is true is to claim only that holding it works. In other words, if believing that fire burns stops you getting burned, then we may say that it is 'true' that fire burns. This will save us the trouble of asking the (pragmatically) meaningless question, 'Does fire *really* burn or not?'

This type of view is a reflection of twentieth-century scientific attitudes. In fact it is the philosophical version of Popper's sophisticated view of scientific procedures, which was mentioned earlier.[3] The pragmatist philosopher merely makes general the scientist's claim that his discoveries are not the discoveries of absolute truths, to be accepted unalterably and without reservation, but simply valuable hypotheses, assumptions that produce useful results when they are made in practice. The nineteenth-century preoccupation of philosophers had been the deduction of absolute eternal truths by a process of pure reasoning unhampered by any appeal to experiment or matters of fact, and pragmatism was to a considerable extent a reaction against this outlook.

Before following up in detail the manner in which Dewey applied this science-based philosophy to education, it may be of value to overlook temporarily the intervening steps and look ahead to the end-product of Dewey's reasoning – the schools which in 1915 he described as 'schools of tomorrow'. The over-all aim of these schools was 'to teach the child to live in the world in which he finds himself'.[4] In practice this ideal, with its implications of flexibility and adaptability, is arrived at by certain distinctive steps which recognisably follow the lines originally suggested by Rousseau. Dewey is very willing to acknowledge his sympathy with Rousseau's ideas, although he describes Emile as 'that exemplary prig.'[5] In particular, Dewey reiterates the child-centred approach: starting from the child, his needs and experiences in planning his education, rather than from what it is thought that adults should know, or from what is traditionally taught in schools. Equally, Dewey accepts the view that development is an unfolding of latent potentialities – a view that is associated with a strong emphasis on developmental stages. But the words which best sum up the procedures of a Dewey school are: *activity*, *discovery* and *freedom*.

LEARNING BY ACTIVITY

The child is encouraged to learn by doing, by activity, since learning is regarded as a process of acting upon things, rather than as a passive process of receiving data through the senses.

Creative activities and other forms of making and doing, will, therefore, take up most of the child's school day, and activity even in the more basic sense of physical movement will be a much more pronounced feature of this type of school than of the traditional school. Not only is sitting rigidly at desks for long periods considered undesirable, but even desks themselves may be dismissed as unnecessary classroom furniture, the ideal classroom being conceived as a well-laid-out workroom. Thus the tendency which both Rousseau and Dewey deplore – that of interposing symbols between facts and the child, whether in the form of words, of books or of maps – would be replaced by as much direct contact as possible between the child and the real world, through actual experiences and the tackling of practical problems.

Dewey is virtually claiming, like a later philosopher, Wittgenstein (51), that 'meaning is use', i.e. that the meaning of a word is the function it fulfils in affecting the behaviour of human beings. Certainly, Dewey believes that a child has only arrived at understanding a word or concept when it fits into a pattern of activities with which he is familiar. This is what he means when he says: 'The things that the child uses in his household occupations, in gardening, in caring for animals, in his plays and games, have real simplicity and completeness of meaning for him. The simplicity of straight lines, angles, and quantities put before him just to be learned is mechanical and abstract.'[6]

DISCOVERY METHODS

The emphasis on activity leads naturally to the use of discovery methods. For instance, instead of early formal instruction in reading, a more oblique approach is used. Every effort is made to stimulate the child's desire to know how to read, in the confidence that what the child *wants* to know he will almost teach himself. The organisation of situations in which the child can discover things for himself leads to an approach which tends to be topic-centred, rather than one which follows traditional subject-boundaries. The 'geography' of America, for instance, was considered by Dewey to embrace the climatic and geological facts, the racial facts, the industrial and political facts, and the social and scientific facts of America.

What he was recommending, therefore, was a complete change:

1. In the subject-matter which was traditionally taught;
2. In the way in which the teacher handled it; and
3. In the way in which the pupils handled it.

In concrete application at the primary level, this meant a school day which might, for instance, include free play in household occupations leading to consideration of the role of perhaps the milkman, the grocer or the postman. The children might then be motivated to pursue further their interest in any one of these. For instance, beginning with the postman, they might go on to find out about his uniform, transportation, the letters he carries, finally finding out about the post office itself, and thus incidentally coming to understand something of the wider world of human relationships in industrial society.

Some of the children might be engaged in cooking. In Dewey's own Laboratory School, there are records of how this occupation led naturally into various fields depending on the age and ability of the children: into science, perhaps, through consideration of the properties of the foodstuffs; into questions of number and measurement; or into the fields of economics and geography through consideration of the sources of the various foods.

There is also, in connection with the Laboratory School, a record of a pupil-built club-house, decorated by the children and then furnished with cushions made of fabrics woven by the children themselves.

These examples show the prime importance which Dewey attached to involving children from the beginning in activities connected with the three basic needs of food, clothing and shelter: needs which will appear valid to even the smallest child.

FREEDOM

Finally, the ideal of freedom meant that for these schools the aim would be the avoidance of prohibitions and commands, and a minimal degree of interference consisting only of preventing the children from interfering with each other. Very often, under the umbrella of an understanding that everyone should be working at something, there would be complete freedom of choice as to what that something should be. Examinations, marks and gradings are rejected, as being not in the spirit of the child/teacher relationship which this type of education aims to establish. In recommending such a degree of freedom, Dewey is not necessarily being unduly naïve as to the nature of children. He says wryly: 'There is much that is "natural" in children which is also naturally obnoxious to adults.'[7] But he is nevertheless confident that an activity-based education can bypass behaviour and discipline problems in a way that traditional, passive, desk-centred education cannot.

PHILOSOPHICAL VIEWS AND EDUCATIONAL THEORY

So far it has not been clear how these educational views relate, as they do, to Dewey's social and political outlook. Although this is more fully discussed in *Democracy and Education* (14), Dewey does indicate the direction of his ideas in *Schools of Tomorrow*. He says:

Education that associates learning with doing will replace the passive education of imparting the learning of others. However well the latter is adapted to feudal societies, in which most individuals are expected to submit constantly and docilely to the authority of superiors, an education which proceeds on this basis is inconsistent with a democratic society where initiative and independence are the rule and where every citizen is supposed to take part in the conduct of affairs of common interest.[8]

Democracy, in other words, means equal participation, and demands an education that trains for equal participation – the kind that involves exercising judgement, for example, and making decisions.

Having looked at the schools which Dewey admired and which in some cases his ideas helped to produce, it is possible to look at those ideas in more detail, bearing in mind the direct relation which Dewey saw between theory and practice. ('Education,' he said, 'is the laboratory in which philosophic distinctions become concrete and are tested.')[9]

It is in *Democracy and Education* that Dewey offers his most systematic exposition of the relationship between his philosophical views and his educational theory.

His philosophical views fall into two broad categories, both of which have already been touched upon. On the one hand, there is his *social* theory, which is democratic and egalitarian; and on the other hand, there is his *epistemological* theory – his views about the nature of knowledge and about what there is to be known.

Democracy and Education relates the individual's education to the type of society that the educator, whether consciously or unconsciously, aims to produce. Like Durkheim, the sociologist, Dewey holds that there are two main alternatives here: either one aims at a traditional and conservative form of society, which will have as its highest value and ideal the preservation of established customs; or, one aims at a progressive changing democratic type of society, in which value is placed on creating the greatest possible variety of mutually shared interests. In the first case, the twin pillars of education will be *custom*, and *authority*. In the second, they will be *interest*, and *freedom*.

It is the latter option that Dewey, as a member of a developing industrial society, advocates. It leads, he argues, to a form of education which is based on the principle of the continuous reorganisation of experience. Most of the earlier part of the book is an explanation of just what is implied by this phrase.

It implies, to begin with, the abandonment of 'teaching by pouring in, learning by passive absorption,' and their replacement by a situation in which the school environment is equipped with 'agencies for doing' – tools and physical materials. In order to fulfil the social purpose of education, though, many of the activities engaged in will be joint activities, which will foster the values of co-operation and mutual working to an objective.

The individual, as opposed to the social end will be personal development and growth, by which Dewey means that the individual's interest in and capacity for further education will be fostered rather than blunted by the education he receives.

Because education relates to a constant reappraisal of present experience, the value of studying the literary products of the past is considerably diminished. Dewey says: 'Isolated from their connection with the present environment in which individuals have to act, they become a kind of rival and distracting environment. Their value lies in their use to increase the meaning of the things with which we have to do at the present time.'[10] Thus both history and literature are to be valued only in so far as they can be seen to bear upon the social problems of the present or the immediate future.

'Problem-centred' approach

In line with this is the recommendation of using intrinsic interest as an alternative to formal discipline; and the idea that interest is best served by introducing activities with immediately comprehensible aims leads to what is termed a 'problem-centred' approach – the setting up of a problem, with guide-lines for its solution, which it is within the child's capacity to follow.

The problem-centred approach is inconsistent with rigid subject divisions, since the solution of a particular problem may depend upon knowledge drawn from several of the traditional areas of knowledge. Moreover, traditional divisions between the subjects have, Dewey holds, been based on the old social order, not the new. It was, he maintains, an education for different social class expectations that led to a distinction between subjects appropriate to a gentleman's education – a liberal education involving literary and artistic studies – and subjects which formed a necessary basis for productive work: practical and vocational studies, which dealt with things rather than ideas. Education in a democratic society, Dewey urges, should do nothing to perpetuate these distinctions.

F

NATURALISM

At this point, it is possible to see the relation between Dewey's social theories and his epistemological views. The opposition between the liberal and the vocational elements in education is held by Dewey to be based on a particular social order – one based on the existence of working and non-working, productive and non-productive classes. Both this dualism and the social order that is symbolised were derived ultimately, Dewey holds, from an original philosophical distinction between the activities of the body and the activities of the mind, the latter having been seen by both Plato and Aristotle as suitable for a ruling class, the former as only suitable for serfs and menials. Philosophy, in its various phases has continued to mirror this original body/mind dualism, with MATERIALISTS (those who believe that body or matter is the only ultimate reality) opposing IDEALISTS (those who believe that mind, or spirit is ultimate). In Dewey's view, this is a false dichotomy, particularly when it is applied at the level of an individual person, who is unnecessarily seen as an association of 'brawn and brain'. In its place, Dewey offers a monistic view very similiar to the behaviourism later propounded by Gilbert Ryle in *The Concept of Mind*. According to this view, mind is not a separate entity, nor do the names of mental faculties, such as judgement, perception and intelligence, refer to things. What they all describe are activities which are the prerogative neither of the body on its own, nor of the mind on its own, but of the person. Not only can man not be artificially divided into mind and body, but also he cannot be separated by this kind of metaphysical gulf from the rest of the universe. Man is, on Dewey's view, himself a part of nature.

This theory, sometimes called NATURALISM, leads directly in two directions: first, to certain views about the nature of knowledge and of learning; and secondly, to a particular view about morals, or values.

Learning is seen as acquiring habits – a process of which both man and other animals are capable. Knowledge, which in the past might have been seen as the end-product of learning, is instead viewed not as something static or merely descriptive, but as something which occurs in action and then becomes a springboard for further action; or, as Dewey puts it, '. . . an outcome of inquiry and a resource in further inquiry.'[11] Thus, the same conclusion is reached by this route as was reached by a consideration of social ends: that the problem-solving situation is absolutely fundamental for man, since he is a biological organism striving to accommodate himself to a largely hostile and destructive environment. In *How we Think* Dewey describes a man arriving at a fork in a path which he hopes will lead him directly to his destination. This situation and the man's attempts to assess the merits of the alternative routes, is seen by Dewey as being typical of all human thinking.

But, of course, this picture of the process of thinking provides a much better model for scientific thought than it does for the arts and the humanities. Hence a scientific view of man led Dewey, not very surprisingly, to a scientific programme for education. It also led him, however, to assimilate everything, including values, to the scientific model.

For Dewey considered that there was no essential difference between a statement of value, and a statement of fact, and that both sorts of statement could be given the same practical appraisal. Just as one can test assumptions about matters of fact by testing out their consequences in the laboratory, so, he thought, value-judgements and moral standards should be assessed in the light of the practical consequences of holding them. Moral ideas should, he felt, be just as much subject to revision as scientific ones.

Experience, then, was all-important in Dewey's thought, since it provides the only possible basis of knowledge. There are, in other words, no unchanging eternal truths, no *a priori* knowledge about the world, of a kind that theologians and philosophers in the past thought possible. On the contrary, the only reality is the reality of man's interaction with his environment.

These ideas link up with Dewey's social theory in that democracy is considered by Dewey to represent the individual's most successful adaptation to his environment – the situation in which the greatest number of individual ends can be satisfied.

CRITICISMS

Dewey's ideas have been widely criticised, not least by himself after a time-lapse of twenty years had revealed the excesses to which over zealous and too uncritical acceptance of his ideas could lead. In *Experience and Education* (15), Dewey offers some justification of the democratic ideal, and supplies some criteria for such concepts as growth and experience, continuity and interaction, which had been missing from his earlier works. These concepts must be looked at both in the light of Dewey's own comments, and also in the light of criticisms made by other writers.

Growth

By far the most important of these concepts, and probably the most ambiguous is 'growth'. In his early writings, Dewey used the term to indicate the most general objective of education for each individual child – laying aside, for the moment, any different social objectives. He also used it, however, as the ultimate justification for a democratic social system (claiming that democracy was the social system under which most 'growth' was possible). In *Experience and Education*, Dewey takes account of the criticism that mere 'growing' is not enough – a child may grow rapidly in a criminal direction, for instance, and – a socially disturbing consideration – left to themselves weeds will do much better in respect of growth than roses. Dewey explains that he regards growth as just one example of the principle of continuity, and that an experience can be regarded as having this quality (continuity) if it arouses curiosity, strengthens initiative, and sets up desires and purposes that are sufficiently intense to carry a person over dead places in the future. An experience has to be judged, he asserts, by reference to what it leads on to. By this criterion, reading, for instance, and speech will be extremely valuable (conducive to growth); constructions from empty cartons perhaps less so.

Useful though this amplification is as a corrective to the school of thought which sees 'growth' as emerging equally from anything which can be called an experience (and *everything* can be called an experience), it does not really answer the objections of Dewey's critics. They were concerned to point out that the use of this term, apparently in a straightforward matter-of-fact sense, concealed in fact a judgement of value. We do actually have to make a judgement as to the direction in which growth should be encouraged, and this will depend, not on scientific knowledge, but on what we consider to be socially acceptable and desirable.

Moreover, even if we accept that the notion of growth is both comprehensible and acceptable as one of the ends of education, there is no reason why it should be set up as the *only* end. In fact, many of the ills of American society have been laid at the door of educationists who made just this assumption: that individual growth, development, self-fulfilment are the only valid aims of the educator. Typical of this sort of criticism is a passage from Berkson's *The Ideal and the Community* in which he says: 'The undertone of antagonism to authority, to traditional belief, to doing right for right's sake is likely to lead to loosening of existing standards rather than raising to a higher mode of conduct. In its lack of confidence in the established order, experimentalism unwittingly casts a shadow of distrust on conventional mores and accepted institutional forms even when these serve valid social purposes.'[12] It is argued, in effect, that given that democracy is desirable as a *social* ideal, it cannot be achieved by democratic schooling; but in the words of C. D. Hardie, 'it may well be that an autocratic school is necessary to establish a democratic world.'[13] Without undertaking an analysis of American society, one can concede that to obtain an ordered society, and even within the society of the school itself, the fulfilment of the individual has always to be balanced against the interests of the social whole.

Social aspects

These criticisms of the social consequences of Dewey's principles, are linked with more general criticisms of the whole concept of a child-centred approach. In *Education in an Industrial*

Society, G. H. Bantock argues that the child is, in any case, totally self-centred, and that it is part of the business of education to extend his horizons and free him from his initial egocentricity.[14]

However, Dewey was by no means blind to the socialising function of education. In fact, it is interesting to contrast these criticisms, which broadly assert that Dewey had too little regard for the social as opposed to the individual ends of education, with other criticisms made from a totally opposite point of view. Because Dewey said such things as: '. . . the teacher is engaged, not simply in the training of individuals, but in the formation of the proper social life' and '. . . through education society can formulate its own purposes, can organize its own means and resources, and thus shape itself with definiteness and economy in the direction in which it wishes to move'[15] it has been suggested that he was virtually recommending indoctrination as an educational policy, and Bantock, who criticises Dewey for his child-centredness, also criticises him for preaching a kind of social conformism which, he says, is on the way to McCarthyism.[16] It must be admitted that in Dewey there is no breath of criticism of mass culture, and no hint of awareness of the value of minorities or of the risk to minorities involved in majority rule.

Nevertheless, at least by the time he wrote *Experience and Education*, Dewey was probably quite as aware as his critics of the narrowness of the path which had to be trod by anyone interested in creating a liberal democratic form of education; the pitfalls on either hand being those of sacrificing individual development to the social order, or alternatively, of unwittingly sabotaging the social order by excessive respect for the individual. It is worth noting, however, that Dewey's educational principles have always been beyond the pale of consideration as far as really repressive and authoritarian political systems have been concerned; one could not imagine them thriving in Communist China, nor was the Nazi régime able to permit the freedom of thinking which they would have engendered. At least to this negative extent Deweyism is historically and logically associated with liberalism, rather than with doctrines of social conformity. To state this, however, is to recognise that wider considerations are at stake than those, merely, of individual growth.

Curriculum

Other criticisms, too, have stemmed from the notion of growth, and the instrumental definition of it which Dewey offered: the fact that Dewey defined growth in terms of continuity, and continuity in terms of experiences leading on to other experiences, meant that he allowed little, if anything, in the school curriculum to be justified for its own sake. As has been noted, this is a criterion which favours scientific studies rather than the humanities; and many critics have been prompted to suggest justifications for the traditional areas of study, and to attack the instrumental conception. Israel Scheffler, for instance, in *Educational Liberalism and Dewey's Philosophy*, suggests that as an educational subject, 'the world in which we live' is altogether too narrow a conception. Human beings, he suggests, are deluding themselves if they believe that they are the centre of the universe. The existence of the human race is, as both astronomy and geology reveal, a mere speck in the universe of time and space. To set as the standard of truth the way in which an idea affects human beings is both arrogant, and, in its widest sense, unscientific. And so, even at the purely practical level of a curriculum for school-children, Scheffler argues that it is ideas which go beyond our own narrow practical environment that best enlarge the intellectual perspectives of the student.

As to the implication of Dewey's theory, that practical studies have far more value than merely theoretical ones, Scheffler argues that this is seeing things the wrong way round. He says:

What is of questionable educational value is trivial, petty, narrow learning, not theoretical study which though illuminating broad reaches of our world, is without practical reference for our own present and future problems. If such study is thus, at least partly, the task of the school, then the school *ought* to stand apart from life in a basis sense: not by cultivating pedantry or myth, but by illuminating a wider world than its limited surroundings and by sustaining those habits of mind which fit it for breadth, penetration, and objectivity of vision.[17]

These remarks need to be supplemented with a comment on the fact that Dewey's criterion was equally destructive to the many activities which come under the general heading of creativity. Writing, painting, modelling, music-making, are all subjects whose value has to be justified in intrinsic terms, and not in terms of what they can lead on to as means to ends.

But in fairness to Dewey, it must be stated that this was an imbalance he tried to some extent to redress in *Experience and Education*. It is significant, though, that in pointing out that history should not be neglected by progressive educationists, he merely underlined his continuing belief that it was the relevance of history to present-day problems that justified its study. In other words, in spite of criticism, he never really questioned the problem-solving model of human learning. And yet problem-solving is only a small part of the activities of human beings, including children, and it is questionable whether it can even be considered the most worthwhile of their activities. In the same year that *Democracy and Education* was published, M. R. Cohen wrote:

What makes human life dignified and worthwhile are not the instrumentalities but certain things which are ends in themselves, the delights of companionship, the joy of creative activity, the vision of beauty, and not least the unique privilege of being for a brief space a spectator of the great drama of existence in which solar systems are born and destroyed – a drama in which our part as actors is of infinitesimal significance.[18]

Method

If these points need to be borne in mind in considering Dewey's aims in education, what modification do they suggest in the methods which Dewey advocated for bringing those aims about?

One important criticism of method needs to be made, and it is one that is made by Dewey himself in *Experience and Education*. The policy of starting from the child's immediate interest is quite incompatible with any systematic approach to teaching; and in many subjects, such as languages, mathematics, or learning to play the piano, a systematic approach is essential because certain fundamentals have to be mastered before any further progress can be made. What is more, whole areas of potentially interesting knowledge may be omitted if the principle of letting the children, rather than the teacher, take the initiative is too rigidly adhered to, and this is a pity since a good teacher can often stimulate children's interest in a subject which it would probably not have occurred to them to inquire about spontaneously. Dewey was prepared to concede, then, that the principle of following the pupil's present interest has to be tempered with consideration of rather more long-term aims and interests.[19]

THE 'LABORATORY SCHOOL'

One final question remains to be considered. To what extent were Dewey's educational ideas as he claimed, scientific? The name 'laboratory school' shows that Dewey regarded the school as a place where ideas about education, the curriculum, child development and levels of interest could be tested out in practice. And no doubt it is true that Dewey and his colleagues had a certain scientific open-mindedness with regard to appraising the success of their policies and ideas. But the hypotheses they entertained were not arrived at initially as a result of attention to research findings; on the contrary, they were largely inspirational and imaginative. This in itself would distinguish their activities from those of other scientists. However, although it is possible that in relation to certain very limited ends, the laboratory school was a place where the means to achieving those ends could be tested out, it is clear that, on the whole, the conception of a laboratory school is mistaken.

The long-term aims of education relate, as Dewey himself was well aware, to life after school. Tests would have to take in a very wide time-span, and careful controls would have to be established to show that the results obtained related to the education received and not to other factors. (These kind of studies are, in fact, being undertaken nowadays.) And even if it were accepted as feasible that short-term experiments could be conducted within a particular school, a genuinely scientific inquiry would need to take account of the many variables involved which could affect results. Every child, for instance, has a different home background, family pattern, inherited character, and so on. But studies of this kind of scientific rigour were not part of Dewey's plan.

The laboratory school, in fact, made its impact not by establishing scientifically any new truths, but by functioning as a show-case for a new set of educational values. It was an opportunity to create a school environment that Dewey and his associates considered *worthwhile*; they believed that, for many children, traditional formal education had been both a misery and a waste of time.

This is a comment which adequately sums up not only the conception of the laboratory school, but all of Dewey's work and writing. It was a crusade for a new set of values in education, rather than, as Dewey himelf conceived it, a new scientific theory of education, and, being a crusade, the measure of its success is the extent to which those values and ideas have been assimilated into subsequent patterns of education both in America and in Europe.

SUMMARY

Dewey followed the thinking of Rousseau and Froebel, and, in America, was associated with the progressive movement in education. He recommended a child-centred approach, aimed at helping the child understand his world and his surroundings. The educational means by which this was to be achieved involved the use of activity and discovery methods, and a maximum of freedom for the child.

Activity and discovery are best promoted, Dewey held, by the avoidance of merely formal instruction, and by supplying within the classroom (and outside it) problem situations and stimuli for investigation.

Because work centres round a problem, traditional subject divisions are avoided in preference to a topic-centred approach. At the primary level, most work of this sort should arise, Dewey thought, from activities connected with supplying the basic needs of food, shelter and clothing.

Dewey held philosophical views concerning society, and also concerning the nature of knowledge. In his social theory, he favours a democratic, progressive and changing order of society, and he argues that the appropriate form of education for this is one which encourages participation, decision-making and experience of working as a member of a group. In his epistemological theory, Dewey regards knowledge, not as a static condition, but as an instrument for further inquiry. He holds a pragmatic or instrumentalist view of truth, which equates truth with usefulness or fruitfulness in future problem-solving activities.

Dewey's views have met with criticism both from himself at a later stage, and from others. (His view that education should be a process of growth has never been adequately defined and defended.) It has also been questioned whether the individualistic free type of education which Dewey recommended is, in fact, that most likely to foster a democratic order of society.

Much criticism has also surrounded the rather narrow view of the curriculum which Dewey's instrumentalism appeared to entail, mainly because it led to a scientific and practical bias at the expense of the humanities.

The principle of starting from the child's interests has also been criticised, if interpreted narrowly to mean that the teacher should not try to *create* interest in what for the child may be initially areas of no interest at all. Dewey himself later recommended taking into account the child's long-term benefit, rather than his immediate present interests.

Dewey's own educational views are best interpreted as judgements as to what is educationally desirable, rather than as scientific judgements supported by such evidence as the experience of his Laboratory School.

NOTES

1. Dewey (17). See introduction by William Brickman, page x.
2. For a full account of this incident, see McCaul, R. L., Dewey, Harper and the University of Chicago, in Brickman and Lehrer (10), page 49.
3. See chapter 2, page 16.
4. Dewey (17), page 123.
5. Dewey (17), page 45.

6. Dewey (17), page 50.
7. Dewey (17), page 76.
8. Dewey (17), page 120.
9. Dewey (14), page 378.
10. Dewey (17), page 80.
11. Dewey (14), page 187.
12. Quoted by Hook, Sidney, in 'John Dewey: His Philosophy of Education and its Critics' in Archambault (1), page 142.
13. See Hardie, C. D. 'The Educational Theory of John Dewey' in Archambault (1), page 124.
14. Bantock (4), page 52.
15. Archambault (1), pages 438–9.
16. Bantock, G. H. *Cambridge Review* (June 1965).
17. See Scheffler, I., 'Educational Liberalism and Dewey's Philosophy' in Archambault (1), page 106.
18. See Cohen, M. R. *New Republic* (8), page 119 (September 1916), quoted by Mason, Robert E., in 'Dewey's Culture Theory and Pedagogy' in Brickman and Lehrer (10), page 121.
19. Dewey (15), pages 78–9.

FURTHER READING

Of Dewey's own writings, priority should be given to reading *Democracy and Education* (14) which is Dewey's most comprehensive exposition of his educational ideas. It would then be illuminating to read the much shorter book, *Experience and Education* (15), in which Dewey deals with criticisms of his earlier work, and makes his own corrections of emphasis. For a short account of the kind of education that Dewey's views entailed, read either *Schools of Tomorrow* (17) or *The Child and the Curriculum* and *The School and Society* (16).

There are a number of collections of selected passages from Dewey's writings, which might be studied either as an alternative to the above or in addition to it, in particular, the collection edited by Garforth (19) or that by Archambault (1).

The collection of critical essays edited by Archambault (2) is strongly recommended. More lengthy works of criticism which might also be consulted are Wirth (50), Baker (3) and Geiger (20).

7 Two Concepts of Education

Consideration of the ideas of these four key figures in educational thought had established a certain pattern. Whereas Rousseau, Froebel and Dewey stand together in their outlook on certain key issues, such as freedom, activity and the central position of the child, Plato alone, representing the Greek tradition, adopts an irreconcilable viewpoint.

Both traditions have had an enormous influence on educational practice, although the progressive trend is the more recent. Both, however, were available for teachers to draw on for their inspiration when education became compulsory, free and widespread in Europe and America.

It may be argued that this is by no means accidental, and that the Platonic view, being only suitable for the education of a wealthy élite, *had* to be replaced by something different once an era of mass education had dawned. This may be true, but there was still a great deal of scope for deciding what that 'something' should be. In England, for instance, at a time when the ideas of Pestalozzi and Froebel were current elsewhere the system which seemed likely to become dominant was not the New Education but the stultifying rote-learning 'monitorial' system of Bell and Lancaster, by which it was claimed that one master could teach a thousand boys.

Even in America, a climate more favourable to the new ideas, a writer who examined the American educational system in 1893 was shocked to find a system which depended on a concept of knowledge as providing fixed answers to set questions. He continues:

The instruction throughout the school consists principally in grinding these answers *verbatim* into the minds of the children. To reach the desired end, the school has been converted into the most dehumanizing institution that I have ever laid eyes upon, each child being treated as if he possessed a memory and the faculty of speech, but no individuality, no sensibilities, no soul.[1]

Schooling in this sense, lacking any intrinsic interest for the child, depended entirely on extrinsic motivation, using merit awards and punishment bands (punishment at first being applied for lack of intelligence, and only later reserved simply for laziness).

This being the established pattern it is remarkable to what an extent the new ideas took over in the mass education area – not, however, ousting the older Platonic tradition in areas where it was deeply rooted (for instance, in the English public schools).

The position now in Great Britain is an interesting one. Examples of each tradition, as well as of the untheoretical straight three Rs tradition, which is not to be identified with either, can be found co-existing in what, geographically, is one educational system. Although the private sphere is perhaps richer in variety and provides examples of the ideas in their most extreme forms, even the state system provides tremendous contrasts of emphasis.

In conclusion, some of these contrasts will be pinpointed and discussed both in relation to earlier thinkers, and to modern viewpoints. These are all issues about which there is continuing controversy, since in no sense has the outcome of any of these disagreements been determined.

The most obvious area in which the contrast between the two notions of education can be seen is that of freedom. As we have seen, advocacy of freedom for the child was historically linked with faith in the basic potentiality for good of the 'free' child; and modern advocates of a maximum of freedom in the upbringing of children (as against an authoritarian approach) echo this attitude. They tend to attribute delinquency and undesirable traits to mishandling or to environmental factors, and indeed it is often children who have already reacted badly to more rigid forms of education who are sent to schools where the emphasis is on freedom.

One of the best-known examples of this approach is Summerhill, the school founded by A. S. Neill. Here the principle of voluntary lessons can be seen carried to its limits, for in his book (33) Neill describes the isolated case of a child who attended the school from the age of seven to seventeen without attending a single lesson, thus showing that 'voluntary' was no mere epithet. Such a policy had as a by-product, of course, some – though not much – illiteracy, and was a handicap to the pupils as far as gaining formal qualifications was concerned. It was Neill's antipathy to books and to learning in a conventional sense, as well as his repudiation of this society and its standards (which he saw as acquisitive and materialistic) that enabled him to discount these disadvantages.

To supporters of more traditional education, though, they seem extremely weighty disadvantages. It seems to them, as it did to Plato, that under these circumstances the child is most probably not becoming acquainted with what is an objective and socially important body of knowledge, one which is there for him to discover given encouragement, and possibly a little compulsion. From their point of view the 'free child' is being allowed to sacrifice his birthright as a civilised human being for a mess of pottage.

In fact, the weight to be attached to these different viewpoints varies in relation to the subject of study which is being considered. Free development of potential is a more attractive proposition in subjects where standards of performance are difficult to assess and where there is no agreed objective measure, such as drama, art or musical appreciation, than it is in the case of, for instance, languages or the sciences. In these subjects there is general agreement as to what constitutes mastery of the subject, and there are clearly recognised things which must be *known* by successful students in those fields. (Of course, there are criteria and standards involved in the first group of subjects, but they are not necessarily *agreed* criteria or standards.) Recognition of this distinction between subjects of study which have objectively right answers, and subjects of study in which the answers are a matter of opinion is, in fact, fundamental in curriculum planning.

Apart from lessons, the question of freedom arises also in

connection with matters of discipline. Here again the extreme progressive view is based to some extent on faith in the likelihood of the child making socially acceptable use of his freedom. Neill at one point suggests that the child brought up to freedom, for instance, will *not* trample on the grand piano, but immediately this clear faith is beset with anomalies. Bitter experience shows Neill that an unlocked workroom at Summerhill will not stay equipped with expensive tools; they will be taken away, lost, or used for any purpose that it occurs to any child to use them for. Since he is not a millionaire, Neill finds he must sanction locks, the antithesis of freedom; and here he reveals his personal hankering after an unattainable educational ideal – no locks, and a millionaire's backing to meet the cost of unrestricted freedom.

The opposite viewpoint, which for obvious economic reasons is reflected in most educational practice, is perhaps best defended by R. S. Peters who suggests that freedom for some children means a life made intolerable for others by peer-group pressures and bullying.[2] William Golding, in *Lord of the Flies*, paints a similar picture of the outcome for children of a life free from the authority and control of adults.

Peters argues that Piaget has shown that children cannot understand the reasons for rules before the age of seven, and that before that age they need to learn to conform to them for reasons of their own safety. Even when old enough to be given a choice, the choice is worthless, he suggests, unless they have already been introduced to the alternatives, by methods which at that stage excluded choice. These opposing attitudes to freedom are to be found in many aspects of the education system. Summerhill, a boarding-school dependent on fees rather than the state for financial support, is best contrasted with other schools in the private sphere, where the view prevails that the purpose of education is to create a certain type of character rather than to foster free development. In the public sector of education, Michael Duane's Risinghill provides a similar contrast to the more conventional day-school which replaced it (5). Outside formal schooling altogether, the views of those who run adventure-playgrounds where fire-lighting, climbing and similar activities are permitted without restriction, are divided by this same stress on the value of freedom from those who see organised games and a framework of rules as the best arrangement for urban youth.

The issue of freedom as opposed to authority is closely related to another issue – that of the relative values of knowledge and experience. The advocates of freedom see freedom as leading to an increase in experience as opposed to formal knowledge, and they regard this as having the greater educational value. Both Rousseau and Dewey made this claim in unambiguous terms. Those who favour a certain amount of authority, however, generally see the authority as providing a framework in which knowledge can be conveyed. The latter group tend to stress that education is a matter of passing on the accumulated knowledge of a culture and civilisation; the former group set greater value on practical skills.

This leads directly to another contrast: that between the liberal view of education, and what has been called its 'therapeutic' trends. The emphasis in the first case is on the subject taught, and it is studied in a disinterested, academic or theoretical fashion – the intrinsic worth of the topic as a subject for study is its justification. In the second case, the starting-point is the child (the learner) and education is seen as a matter of meeting his needs and interests so as to foster the development of his personality in a psychologically satisfying way. Of course, although this is the *aim* of this type of education, there is little evidence to show that the methods used achieve these aims, any more than that the academic approach always results in a child's full appreciation for, or love of, a particular subject of study.

To an increasing extent this conflict is reflected in the varying approaches to primary and secondary education. The organisational structure of primary and secondary schools is itself an aspect of this difference. In the primary schools, the stress on pastoral care of children is made easier by a framework in which one teacher is responsible for every aspect of the work of a single group of children for a whole year. (Team teaching is a new development which, to some extent, will alter this picture if it is widely adopted.) In secondary schools, on the other hand,

G

the child's day and experience is fragmented by contact with different specialist teachers. Until the decision to introduce widespread comprehensive schooling was taken, it seemed that the child-centred primary approach would gradually be taken over into at least the lower forms of the secondary modern schools, leaving the grammar schools comparatively unaffected, and thus deepening the gulf already existing between the 'child-centred' and the 'subject-centred' approach. The Newsom Report, with its recommendation for the less academic approach to the education of secondary school children of average and below-average ability, tended to reinforce this trend. It is possible, however, that a comprehensive system may serve to bring these extremes closer together. Whether this can be done, or whether the needs of a technological society for highly educated and specialised manpower will ensure that the dichotomy is maintained, is something which the next ten or twenty years may determine as far as the British educational scene is concerned.

The solution to this problem is closely linked with that of another: integration of studies. It is often thought that the subject specialist is likely to have a vested interest in the preservation of narrow subject boundaries, while the progressive non-specialist can clearly see that these are the result of purely artificial and misleading divisions. Several of the newer universities, however, have shown that specialists themselves may be among those most interested in fostering interdisciplinary studies where these are a viable possibility – although here it must be remembered that interdisciplinary studies are in a sense parasitic on specialisms, in that the teaching of the contributory disciplines is nearly always in the hands of specialists in the discipline.

At the primary level, the position is reasonably straightforward: with one teacher in charge of all the studies of a class, and confidently ahead of the class in any discipline they care to touch upon, it may well be more interesting, as well as more convenient, to have subjects stemming from a topic rather than following appointed spaces on the time-table. But even at this level it is becoming recognised that, for instance, the systematic study of a foreign language cannot be approached in this way; and that even here there are specialisms, e.g. music or science, which are best taught by people with special knowledge or interest – hence the growth of support for the team-teaching concept.

But it is important to notice that whatever conclusion we come to on the subject of integration of studies – whether, like Plato, we regard the logical structure of knowledge as the essential determinant of any educational venture, or follow such educationists as Froebel and Dewey in stressing the interrelatedness of the different aspects of knowledge – it has to be recognised that the views of these earlier thinkers on this particular subject have little relevance to the later twentieth century. The vast increase in knowledge and development of disciplines, including the evolution of new ones, such as experimental psychology and sociology, all present us with a totally new situation from which to take stock of the arguments for and against integration of studies.

Freedom, integration and the learner-oriented approach are concepts which tend to be developed as an interdependent group by their supporters in education. Another vitally important issue which seems to fall outside this framework altogether is that of equality. As we have seen, Dewey linked the objective of fostering social equality to that of freedom, where Froebel, by contrast, had been concerned to assure critics that freedom in education would not lead to any process of social levelling. Plato, as we have seen, did not acknowledge the value of either ideal. What seems clear is that Dewey's difficulties in reconciling the aims of social equality and free development were no mere accident. In the political sphere, de Tocqueville (49) had earlier argued that freedom and equality were irreconcilable aims, and that every step in the direction of social equality meant an inroad into personal freedom. And indeed, it is now a commonplace that in politics we make a choice about the balance we want to accept between these two ideals.

In education it is not surprising that there is difficulty in reconciling, for instance, the principle of allowing the child freedom in respect of what and whether he learns, with the determined organisation of non-voluntary social studies courses and social training for him, although both these programmes tend to be put forward by the same people. Nor is it surprising that a similar conflict should arise between the demand that there should be freedom for variety and experiment in education, and the demand that equality should be pursued by the removal of privilege, either in the form of fee-paying education or in the form of schools restricted to a single high-ability range.

As in the political sphere, the only valid comment to be made here is that progress can only be achieved by the recognition that there *are* alternative ideals, that more freedom *does* mean less equality, and vice versa, and that the task to be faced is not one of reconciling irreconcilables, but of reaching (probably by compromise) agreement within the educational system on the balance between the two ideals.

Like the other issues this may reasonably be termed an unresolved and perennial problem – perennial in the sense that every generation reaches its conclusions afresh on the issue. This means that on these broad general issues of principle, the arguments and viewpoints of the educational theorists we have considered here have as much claim to our attention as contemporary viewpoints – which, indeed, repeat them to an astonishing extent. This brings us to the question of the status of the theories put forward by these thinkers. Were they, or were they not, educational theories in the sense suggested in chapter 2?

The answer to this question has already been foreshadowed in relation to Dewey who, it was claimed, presented a 'showcase of educational values'.[3] This same description applies equally to the other educational theorists who have been considered here. In each case a strong value-element predominates. That is to say, they have not, in general, taken certain ends for granted, and then offered guidance based on empirical evidence as to how those ends might best be achieved. On the contrary, they set out for acceptance or rejection, the ends for which the educationist should aim.

To admit that what they have offered has been, to some extent, a personal viewpoint as opposed to a scientific theory, is not necessarily to undermine their contribution. In fact, had they offered theories in the sense of testable hypotheses then they would have had very little to contribute to the problem of educating the child of today. For if educational ends were established beyond question, then the most satisfactory methods for achieving those ends could best be worked out by applying the results of the most recent and up-to-date researches of psychologists and sociologists; and the kind of inspired guesswork which these earlier theorists brought to bear on practical problems could safely be ignored by the practising teacher. But looking at the contemporary educational scene, it is clear that educational ends are by no means established much beyond these limits except in so far as certain basic well-established parts of the curriculum, such as the three Rs, are generally accepted in any modern industrial society, as being necessary to make the ordinary person in that society reasonably socially efficient. As we have seen, the differing ends assumed by the thinkers who have been discussed here are still assumed by some, denied by others, yet continue to determine patterns of education in different parts of the educational scene. These very complex statements of aim, then, although historical rather than contemporary, are very relevant to any serious present consideration of educational ends.

One final question remains to be discussed. In each case, the educational ideas of these thinkers have been linked with a much broader general philosophical position. Nevertheless, it would be a mistake to suppose that the educational views *follow from* the philosophical position in any strict logical sense. For one thing, it is logically impossible that they should, for philosophical propositions are themselves neither value-judgements nor empirical statements. This means that they cannot serve as evidence for educational views, since these can only be understood either, as has been suggested here, as value-judgements, or, as their defenders have sometimes thought, as empirical judgements. In neither case could they be held to follow from statements of a logical analytic or *a priori* form, but only from statements of the same logical type as themselves.

This relationship is ruled out, then, on logical grounds. It will be clear to the reader, however, that it is also ruled out on other grounds. The philosophy of Froebel, for instance, was metaphysical and idealistic, while that of Dewey was, in complete contrast, empiricist and materialistic. But these two completely opposed philosophical views did not prevent their authors contributing to the same trend in education; while Plato, who was also an idealist and metaphysician had nothing at all in common with the educational outlook of Froebel.

Nevertheless, it is true that the two trends have loose philosophical associations although these are not of a strictly logical nature. The tradition initiated by Rousseau, with its emphasis on freedom and individuality, is in fact associated with a much broader general philosophy: a philosophy whose political aspect is liberal democracy and whose epistemological aspects are empiricism, materialism and pluralism.

The Platonic tradition, on the other hand, is associated with an authoritarian political structure, with respect for tradition, and with an idealistic rather than a materialist epistemological outlook. In both cases, however, the correlations are extremely inexact, and the link is only a matter of contingent fact and by no means necessary. This means that the contemporary Platonist in education, for instance, is in no sense *committed* to either idealism in philosophy or to authoritarianism in politics. Similarly, there is nothing inconsistent in the behaviour of a theist or indeed a mystic in advocating Dewey's practical approaches to education.

Educational policy has been presented here as largely a matter of choice; and consideration of the views of those who have most strongly advocated a particular path is one way of making our present choices informed rather than merely casual. It is, however, by no means the only way. In making their own choices, these thinkers had scant regard for the non-obvious facts about children which contemporary studies have revealed. The process of child development was gauged in general terms from unregulated observation; learning was aimed at, but without any scientific knowledge of the learning process; individual differences were submerged under the weight of general and universal theories; and the effects of social background and of social and cultural influences remained unrecognised and unconsidered by thinkers whose ideas preceded the large-scale collection of data which has been a comparatively recent feature of educational research.

Today's judgements can be made on a greatly more informed basis than was possible for the thinkers who instituted the main trends in education – a point which Dewey himself recognised when considering the question of education as a study. He said, 'It is not a matter of crude speculation nor of doling out arbitrary empiric devices, but of getting together a definite sphere of historical, sociological, and economic facts, and of combining these facts with others drawn from physiology, hygiene, and medicine, etc., and of effecting a working synthesis on this great range of scientific data.'[4] What Dewey failed to recognise was that the data themselves could not determine any conclusions. The question of the relation between data and conclusions, and that between beliefs (concerning the data) and attitudes (as evinced in conclusions as to what ought to be done) has been the subject of much recent discussion in moral philosophy. For example, Stevenson, in *Ethics and Language*, uses the example of the problem of trustees of a wealthy benefactor, who wonder whether to use his endowment to benefit hospitals or universities, to demonstrate that it is attitude which is the more fundamental – agreement about beliefs can in principle be reached eventually, but a difference in attitude can persist after all factual differences have been resolved.[5]

Similarly, in education, having established the facts as far as we are able, it remains the case that we must determine the ends and objectives for ourselves. However, the wider the range of empirical data with which we are acquainted, the more adequately we can do this, and it is on the basis of these wider data that any future educational theories which are to win acceptance must be founded.

SUMMARY

Plato on the one hand and Rousseau, Froebel and Dewey on the other, belong to two contrasting educational traditions which are reflected in divergent trends in education today.

Among the key-issues in which these differences of opinion manifest themselves are the issues of freedom as opposed to authority,

experience as opposed to knowledge, liberal as opposed to 'therapeutic' aims in education, specialisation as opposed to integration of
studies, and the issue of equality.

The educational theorists offered a personal viewpoint on many of
these issues, and recommended the pursuit of particular educational
ends. Although their recommendations on education were linked with
particular philosophical viewpoints, they are in fact independent of
them. They are also strictly (or logically) independent of empirical
facts and evidence, but nevertheless it must be recognised that the
relative poverty of factual data with which they were acquainted
imposed inevitable limits on the value of their conclusions. We have
to decide to adopt or reject their different points of view in the light
of the wider knowledge that is now available to us.

NOTES

1. From Joseph Mayer Rice, *The Public School System of the United
   States* (The Century Co. (N.Y.) 1893), quoted in Wirth (50), page
   31.
2. Peters (36), chapter VII.
3. Chapter 6, page 90.
4. See Dewey, John, 'Pedagogy as a University Discipline', *University
   Record* (1) No. 26 (September 1896), quoted in Wirth (50), page 42.
5. Stevenson (45), pages 11–19.

FURTHER READING

For a description and justification of an English school following
'freedom' principles see Neill (33). Berg (5) gives a description of
what has been controversially construed as an attempt to introduce
some of the same ideas into the running of a non-boarding state
secondary school. A book which incorporates some defence of
alternative ideals (in the process of defending the grammar-school
against the threat of comprehensivisation) is Davis (13). For a philosophical discussion of arguments relating to both types of ideal, see
Peters (36), particularly Part 2.

The ethical distinction between beliefs and attitudes is presented
and discussed in Stevenson (45), chapter 1.

Bibliography

Books

1. Archambault, R. D. (Ed.) *John Dewey on Education, Selected Writings* (Random House – The Modern Library (USA) 1964)
2. Archambault, R. D. (Ed.) *Dewey on Education, Appraisals* (Random House (USA) 1966)
3. Baker, Melvin C. *Foundations of John Dewey's Educational Theory* (Atheling Books (USA) 1965)
4. Bantock, G. H. *Education in an Industrial Society* (Faber 1963)
5. Berg, L. *Risinghill, Death of a Comprehensive* (Penguin 1968)
6. Boyd, W. *Emile for Today* (Heinemann 1956)
7. Boyd, W. *Introduction to the Republic of Plato* (Allen & Unwin 1911)
8. Boyd, W. *Plato's Republic for Today* (Heinemann 1962)
9. Boyd, W. *The Minor Educational Writings of J. J. Rousseau* (Blackie 1911)
10. Brickman, W. W. & Lehrer, S. (Eds.) *John Dewey: Master Educator* (Atherton (USA) 1965)
11. Cornford, F. M. *The Republic of Plato* (Oxford University Press 1941)
12. Curtis, S. J. & Boultwood, M. E. A. *A Short History of Educational Ideas* (University Tutorial Press 1966)
13. Davis, R. *The Grammar School* (Penguin 1967)
14. Dewey, J. *Democracy and Education* (The Free Press (USA) 1966)
15. Dewey, J. *Experience and Education* (Collier Books (USA) 1966)
16. Dewey, J. *The Child and the Curriculum* and *The School and Society* (University of Chicago Press – Phoenix Books 1956)
17. Dewey, J. & E. *Schools of Tomorrow* (Dutton (USA) 1962)
18. Field, G. C. *The Philosophy of Plato* (Oxford University Press 1949)
19. Garforth, F. W. (Ed.) *John Dewey, Selected Educational Writings* (Heinemann 1966)
20. Geiger, G. R. *John Dewey in Perspective* (McGraw-Hill (USA) 1964)

21. Hailmann, W. N. *Froebel, The Education of Man*, an abridged translation (Appleton (USA) 1887)

22. Jarvis, J. (Ed.) *Froebel's Pedagogics of the Kingdergarten* (E. Arnold 1899)

23. Lawrence, E. (Ed.) *Friedrich Froebel and English Education* (University of London Press 1952)

24. Liddell, R. *Some Principles of Fiction* (Cape 1953)

25. Lilley, I. M. *Friedrich Froebel, A Selection from his Writings* (Cambridge University Press 1967)

26. Lodge, R. C. *Plato's Theory of Education* (Kegan Paul 1947)

27. Lodge, R. C. *The Philosophy of Plato* (Routledge & Kegan Paul 1956)

28. Lovell, K. *Educational Psychology and Children* (University of London Press. Ninth edition 1967)

29. Marshall, S. *An Experiment in Education* (Cambridge University Press 1966)

30. Mayhew, K. C. & Edwards, A. C. *The Dewey School* (Appleton-Century (USA) 1945)

31. Michaelis, E. & Moore, H. K. *Autobiography of Friedrich Froebel*, translated and annotated (Sonnenschein 1886)

32. Musgrave, P. W. *The Sociology of Education* (Methuen 1965)

33. Neill, A. S. *Summerhill* (Gollancz 1966)

34. Nettleship, R. L. *Lectures on the Republic of Plato* (Macmillan 1962)

35. O'Connor, D. J. *An Introduction to the Philosophy of Education* (Routledge & Kegan Paul 1957)

36. Peters, R. S. *Ethics and Education* (Allen & Unwin 1966)

37. Popper, K. *The Logic of Scientific Discovery* (Hutchinson 1956)

38. Popper, K. *The Open Society and its Enemies*, Vol. 1 (Routledge 1945)

39. Rousseau, J. J. *Emile* (Dent–Everyman 1966)

40. Rousseau, J. J. *Julie ou la Nouvelle Heloise* (Harrap 1967)

41. Rousseau, J. J. *The Social Contract* and *Discourses* (Dent–Everyman 1955)

42. Rusk, R. R. *The Doctrines of the Great Educators* (Macmillan. Third edition 1965)

43. Schillp (Ed.) *The Philosophy of John Dewey* (Northwestern University (USA) 1939)

44. Sealey, L. G. W. & Gibbon, V. *Communication and Learning in the Primary School* (Blackwell 1962)

45. Stevenson, C. L. *Ethics and Language* (Yale University Press 1944)

46. Talmon, J. L. *The Origins of Totalitarian Democracy* (Mercury Books–Secker & Warburg 1961)

47. Tanner, J. M. *Education and Physical Growth* (University of London Press 1961)

48. Taylor, A. E. *Plato – The Man and his Work* (Methuen 1926)

49. Tocqueville, A. de *Democracy in America* (Faber 1958)

50. Wirth, Arthur G. *John Dewey as Educator* (Wiley (USA) 1966)

51. Wittgenstein, L. *Philosophical Investigations* (Blackwell. Third edition 1967)

Articles

52. Hirst, P. 'Philosophy and Educational Theory', *Brit. J. Educ. Stud.*, **XII** (1) (November 1963)

53. MacMurray, F. 'Preface to an Autonomous Discipline of Education', *Educational Theory* 5 (3) (1955)

Index